BIO-DEMOGRAPHIC STUDY OF KASHMIRIS

BIO-DEMOGRAPHIC STUDY OF KASHMIRIS

KANAN K. SADHU

Gian Publishing House

29/6 SHAKTI NAGAR · DELHI-110007 · INDIA

GIAN PUBLISHING HOUSE
29 / 6, SHAKTI NAGAR, DELHI - 110007

ISBN 81-212-0072-5

PRINTED IN INDIA

Printed by Mrs. Gayatri Garg for Gian Publishing House, Delhi-110007 and Printed by Shri Dhar Bhatt for Kalyani Printers (Composing Unit), Delhi-110035

Foreword

In recent years changes of vast magnitudes are affecting the distribution, population density and way of life of human populations all over the world. It is important today to study the demographic structure and population biology of human communities because here the consequences of bio-social interactions are remarkably perceptible. It is only during the last few decades that we have become progressively aware to the problems relating to fertility and the bio-social factors affecting it.

The primary intention of this book is to show the extent of diversity in the bio-demographical patterns of the Kashmiri populations which may have been incorporated due to change in the socio-economic status and exposure to changed environment. Dr. (Mrs.) Kanan Kusum Sadhu has made a significant contribution by demonstrating effect of maternal constitution on their fertility performance and also relationship of physique of mother and sex ratio of their children among the Kashmiri Pandits and Muslims. The study assumes further significance as very little information is available on the population dynamics of the Kashmiri people of semi-urban as well as of urban origin.

The sex ratio as an indicator of the relative number of males and females in a population is a basic measure in demography and genetics. The author calls the Kashmiri population as 'masculine in character'. Among all the Kashmiri populations under study, the desired average number of sons is much higher than the daughters in both categories of parents those using birth control devices and those not using birth control devices. If the same populations are examined for different historic periods, there is, as one would expect, a general tendency within the recent past to form a distinct mendelian group and this seems to have occurred among the Kashmiri population.

I am very pleased to recommend this book to the students of Anthropology in particular and other readers in general.

PROF. (DR.) S. C. TIWARI

Professor & Head
Department of Anthropology
University of Delhi
Delhi-110007

Preface

The valley of Kashmir, which has been called paradise on earth and which is surrounded by the mountain ranges of North Western Himalayas, is inhabited by one ethnically homogeneous population comprising Pandits and Muslims. These two population groups share common heritage and common history, yet over the last six centuries they have come to differ from each other in faith, customs and many other aspects. Investigations were made to determine to what extent changes in socio-religio-economic status and the physical environment has diversified the bio-demographic pattern of these two groups. In the course of this investigation, I have made comparative study of these two religion based communities in the matter of demographic structure and population biology. I have also observed that so far the rural urban differenciation in bio-demographic patterns has mainly attracted the anthropologists. In the modern India. due to economic and other factors, the population composition has been undergoing considerable change with the result that Semi-urban populations have started swelling in number. While making comparative studies, I have, therefore, selected representative urban and semi-urban population sample. Another factor which I could not overlook was the fact that in the post Independence India, Delhi, the capital of our country, has become the second largest concentration of Kashmiri population. It was, therefore, felt necessary to study the effects of this changed environment as well. Further an assessment has also been made of the association that may exist between fertility and body dimensions among the two population groups to reveal the differentiations, if any.

This study was basically undertaken to present thesis to the

University of Delhi which has awarded me the degree of Ph.D. The late Prof. P.K. Datta was my guide for this work and I remember with gratitude the guidance provided by him in this field. I am also grateful to Dr. A.K. Kalla who so painstakingly went through chapter after chapter of this book and gave me valuable suggestions for its improvement. I would also wish to express my gratitude to all those in the Department of Anthropology of the University of Delhi who provided me with encouragement, assistance and guidance. My special thanks are due to Prof. S. C. Tiwari, Head of the Department for kindly writing a foreword for this book.

C 1/79, Ashok Vihar II,
Delhi-110052
November, 1986

KANAN K. SADHU

Contents

CHAPTER

1

Bio-Demographic Studies : An Introduction

'Demography,' says Donald, J. Bogue (1969) "is the mathematical and statistical study of the size, composition and spatial distribution of human population and of changes in these aspects through the operation of the five processes of fertility, mortality, marriage, migration and social mobility. Although it maintains a continuous description and comparative analysis of trends in each of these processes and in their net result, its long run goal is to develop theories to explain the events that it charts and compares".

The study of human population and the various trends has shown the twin objectives of lower morality and lower fertility. On the one hand lower mortality is a universally desired and accepted social goal and on the other hand lower fertility and the means for achieving it have long been subjects of religious controversy and of ethical, social and individual debate. Stolnitz (1964) is of the view that downward trends in fertility require a shift in attitudes from the traditional fatalism typical of peasant societies to a positive belief that one's destiny can be affected by one's deeds, in child bearing as in other spheres of behaviour. The lower mortality can be achieved by planned public health, sanitation, mass medical programmes, spread of education and improved economic conditions.

In the context of the explosive growth of population, the term 'Population Explosion' has often been used. This according to Freedman (1964) is less accurate. While the size of population growth is vital in itself, there are many other aspects of structure and change in populations which are equally important. The world population is now largest in history (about 4.5 billion) and is rising at an average annual rate of 6.6 million people (Census of India—1981 Provisional figures). Yet the question to be decided is whether the world should be considered as a whole or major continents and regions separately. There is a wide ranging diversity in the present day world between the rich and the poor, the developed and the developing, the industrialized and the aggrarian. It is, therefore, feasible to study the situation specific to specific sections or groups.

India is the world's second most populous country next only to China and about 15.53% of the world's population lives in this sub-continent whereas it has just 2.4 per cent of the world area (1981 census, Provisional figures). Currently a phase of accelerating growth of population is being experienced in this country not because there is any sudden glut in the fertility rate but because of appreciable decline in the mortality rate; from 47.2 per thousand in 1911-20 to 27 4 in 1941-50 and down to 14.8 in 1981. The population has grown from 252 million in 1911 (for undivided India) to 361 million in 1951, 547.9 million in 1971 and 683.8 million in 1981 (Census, 1981). Bhattacharjee and Shastri (1976) have divided the current century into three broad periods on the basis of the rates of population growth; 1901 to 1921, 1921 to 1951 and 1951 onwards. During the first phase, from 1901 to 1921, the growth rate of population was very low (population increase from 238.3 million to 251.2 million). During the second phase, 1921 to 1951, the growth rate was eight-fold (from 251.2 to 361 million). In the third phase beginning 1951. the growth rate has been steady but rising. It grew from 361 million to 684 million as at present.

In 1951 a birth rate of 43 per thousand was reported and thanks to the massive family planning programme launched by the Government of India this rate has declined. (It was 38 in 1971, 35 in 1974 and 33 in 1978). This in itself is no mean achievement but this has been offset to a great extent by lower mortality. There has been a decline in the death rate from 47.2 per thousand in 1911-20 to 15.9 in 1969-70. The death rate in 1971 was 15.7 per 1000 and in 1981 it was only 14.8 per 1000 (Census of India). Consequently, India's population is expanding at an alarming rate and if this rate continues unchecked the present population may be doubled within the next three and odd decades.

Malthusian theory of population was a landmark in the study of population problem. An improvement to this theory was that of the exponents of optimum population. In the modern times biological theories about population have received considerable attention. It is sought to explain that human beings are no different from animals in the matter of living and dying. Some of the important theories are (*i*) M.T. Sadler's Density & Fecundity Principal) (*ii*) Doubleday's Diet Theory, (*iii*) Raymond Pearl and Lowell J. Reed's Logistic Curve Theory, (*iv*) Corrado Ginis Theory of Biological Stages, (*v*) Herbert Spencer's Analysis of Fertility Function and (*vi*) Jouse de Castro's theory of Protein Consumption. These theories have provided the bases for the study of biological factors affecting fertility. The study of chromosomes in relation to still births and child mortality has been carried out by Penrose (1964), Court Brown et al (1969), Bauld et al (1974) and Machin and Crolla (1974) etc.

Only one-fifth period of the present century is left and we in India have already crossed the 683 million mark in population. The average density per sq. km. is 221 while it is as high as 4,178 in Delhi. Women are still out numbered by men, there being 935 women to every 1000 men. More and more people are moving from rural to urban areas and our cities are bursting at the seams. The literacy rate today is 36.17 per cent (average) —46.74% (for men) and 16.67% (for women). The rate of growth during 1971-81 decade has been 24.75% which is marginally lower than 24.80% during the 1961-71 decade. (Census of India, 1971 and 1981). The increase in our population during 1971-81 has been more than the addition over first half of the present century and the population has thus nearly doubled since India got independence.

The death rate has reduced to 14.8 per thousand, longevity has increased to 54 years, we are self-sufficient in food-grains and are among 10 most industrialised nations ln the world and yet 48% of our population is living below the poverty line. To meet this challenge the Health Minister of India while conferring at New Delhi on 22-10-81 with the Indian delegation for Asian Conference of Parliamentarians on Population and Development, stated that 'on the basis of the various measures being taken by the Government of India, it is hoped that India would attain zero rate of population growth by 2050 A.D.'

Gupta (1974) has conducted a study of the variation in the age-structure of Indian population during sixties. The Planning Commission of India (1979) has pointed out a special feature of the projected Indian Population viz., a sharp increase in the age-group 15-59 from about 54% in 1978 to about 59% in 1991. It implies that even if the age-specific fertility rates remain constant, the birth rates would increase just because of structural change, and the death rate would diminish, resulting in upward trend in natural growth rate.

Masnick and McFalls Jr. (1976) have thrown light on the new perspective in the twentieth century American fertility swing. A variety of factors, according to them, determine the desired family size in modern America, these include social variables like neighbourhood composition and demand on health and educational system. Since child bearing can take place over the entire reproductive period of a woman, therefore, the elements throughout this period determine the child birth, number and their spacing. One has, therefore, to adopt a cohort perspective on fertility which makes our study and approach more realistic. The elements include socio-economic correlates of fecundability. A study of this in a sample of Taiwanese women was carried by Jain (1969).

It would not be out of place to mention biological factors determining sex of the offspring which ultimately decides the sex-ratio in a community. Various cytological studies suggest that human sperms are of two kinds with reference to sex determinant and that these two kinds are produced in equal numbers. If these deductions are assumed as correct and if other factors are constant, one would expect a sex ratio of 50:50 between live birth males and females. In actual practice it is not so. One would say that this may be due to larger number of female embryo deaths. But the fact is that there are more male still births at every period of gestation. The possible explanations are (*i*) the male sperms are more mobile to reach upper ends of the oviduct in time to fertilize the eggs; (*ii*) the female determining sperms are more vulnerable to lethal genetic factors and (*iii*) female sperms have lower survival value in chemical environment of the female genital tract (Strandskov, 1942). In this connection the two studies carried out in 1976 are noteworthy (*a*) by Frisancho et al the symbolic relationship of high fertility, high childhood mortality and socio-economic status in urban Peruvian population and (*b*) by Verbrugge, on the sex differentials in morbidity and mortality in the United States. The other important studies on the sex-ratio are of Kang and Cho (1962), Hunt Jr. et al (1965), Cross and McKusick (1970), Morland Yan (1975) and Jain (1975).

India as a developing country has drawn up a national population policy which is stated to stand somewhere between pessimistic prediction of the neo-Malthusians that mankind, particularly the third world, is heading for a major disaster, and the assumption of the structuralists who are convinced that the earth's resources are sufficient to cope with any size of population provided society can be restructured in such a way as to ensure the universal application of ever-advancing technological progress (Epstein, 1975). This population policy was termed by India's Health Minister in the World Population Conference held at Bucharest in August 1974 "as an instrument for securing comprehensive social development". He added that "this instrument cannot be effective unless certain concomitant economic policies and social programmes succeed in changing the basic determinants of high fertility"—for mortality cannot and should not rise now because of better conditions of living. Hence, the study of fertility has been gaining increasing importance in the recent past.

In 1952, the Government of India was the first among the few governments in the world to adopt family planning as a national policy. The aim was to contain the birth rate. This has given added importance to the study of fertility and its orientation to related official programmes and policies. The family planning programmes are directed towards striking a balance between the economic imputs and the number required to be fed by these. Stoeckel and Choudhury (1969) and Wright (1975) have conducted studies in Bangladesh and the United States respectively. In her paper Williamson (1980) has discussed the means of utilising research to manage a family planning project. Kumari and Rao (1982) have discussed association between family planning and fitness of the child to survive. Hernandez (1981) has analysed the independent impact of family planning programmes on fertility and Srikantam and Saxena (1981) have discussed the population census results with special reference to the state intervention in reducing fertility, in the form of family planning programme.

India started the family planning programme right from the first five year plan. The outlay during the first plan period 1951-56 was a modest Rs. 6.5 million which was increased to a sizeable outlay of Rs. 5160 million in the fifth plan period 1974-79. There are 5132 main centres (with 33,370 sub centres) in the rural areas and 1975 centres in urban areas for providing family planning advice, and service. It is estimated that during the 15 years, 1961 to 1975 as many as 20.5806 million births were averted with the help of sterilisation, I.U.D.* and C.C.** usage and other family planning devices. By March 1980 the percentage of couples protected by these devices had risen to 22.6 million (Shrikantam and Saxena, 1981).

What has come to stay as an important factor having impact on the population growth is the desire for children and the preference for their sex. This in itself is also influenced by social attitudes and individual preferences. Some of the important works on attitude to family size and sex preferences are those of Novitski and Kimball (1958), Pareek and Kothandapani (1969), Raina (1969),

*Intra uterine devices

**Conventional contraceptives

Gustavus and Nam (1970), Cutright *et al* (1974), Stinner and Madar (1975), Talwar (1975) and Coombs (1979). In spite of the initial aggressive protests against abortion from some sections of various communities, the medical termination of pregnancy is more and more being adopted as an important tool for restricting the number of children. In 1979-80, by Sept., 1979 as many as 1·47 lakh such operations had been carried out. Naylor (1974)) has analysed the relation between spontaneous abortion and maternal age, parity and pregnancy compensation artifact etc. Likewise Potter et. al (1975) have discussed the competition between the spontaneous and induced abortion along with inter pregnancy intervals, competing pregnancy outcomes and a hypothesis for a negative association between incidences of abortion and miscarriage based on a study in Taiwan.

Demographers have drawn a distinction between fecundity and fertility. According to Thompson and Lewis (1965) fecundity is a biological potential—the physiological capacity to participate in reproduction, whereas fertility is the actual reproductive performance of a woman or a group of women. The population analysits are, therefore, obviously concerned with the latter. The fertility behaviour is affected by biological factors and personal preferences directly and social customs and collective preferences indirectly. All these bio-social factors have, therefore, to be taken into account while formulating the population policy of a country.

Fertility may be defined as the number of births occurring in a population unit during a specified time period which is the period between menarche and menopause. Hence, a woman is said to be fertile if ever she has borne a live child (Jones, 1974). Several attempts have been made to study the fertility among various populations in India. In 1911 the first official enquiry was made by Census of India. The data collected then and afterwards in 1921 and 1931 censuses were confined to small areas only (Agarwala, 1966). Jain (1939) gave the relationship between fertility, social status and economic conditions. Chandrasekharan (1948) identified Parsis as having low fertility. In 1951 Davis presented a fertility background of the population in India and Pakistan in relation to the socio-demographic characteristics. Dandekar and Dandekar (1953) did a study of the pattern of fertility and of rural-urban difference in Poona. Sovani and Dandekar (1955) analysed the attitudes of people towards family planning. Different studies were conducted on the fertility by Sinha (1957) in Uttar Pradesh and Rakshit (1962), Bhowmik and Bhowmik (1967) and Bhowmik and Chowdhuri (1970) in the eastern part of the country. Chandrasekhar (1961) is of the opinion that hetrogenous character of Indian population is an obstacle in formulating plans for the restriction of fertility rate. Ghosh (1975), while reviewing the various studies done on fertility, has observed that the fertility is boradly an outcome of the interaction between fecundity and the desire for children. Fecundity is the latent capacity for the re-producing and is an attitude of couples. In populations, however, fecundity can be crudely indicated by the distribution of women between the ages of menarche and menopause i.e., 15 to 49 (15 to 44 according to Stein and Sussex, 1975).

Fertility has been studied in many an aspect the world over. Johnston et. al. (1969) have discussed interrelationship of demography, genetics and culture on the basis of the population structure of Peruvian Cashinahna. Karan and Boerner (1973) have analysed spatial pattern of human fertility behaviour in India. Study on Argentine fertility was carried out by Cicourel (1974). While Halberstein and Crawford (1975) have presented the demographic structure of Tlaxcalan population in Mexico, McAlpine and Simpson (1976) have discussed the demographic and fertility aspects of Canadian Eskimos. Studies in New Orleans conducted by Harter in 1970 and in Afghanistan by Trussell and Brown in 1979 are also important. Fertility in relation to spacing of births has been studied by Yerushelony (1945), Freedman and Coombs (1966), Grabill and Davidson (1968), Bhanot and Gandotra (1970) and Khan (1973). The aspect relating to timing of first birth in Maheshwari community is given in his paper by Gandhi (1978) and in general by Presser (1971). Fertility and Genetics is the subject of the works of Oliveira and Salzano (1969), Scott-Emuakpor (1974), Crawford and Gmelch (1974), Lee and Lin (1974).

Roberts and Lowe (1975) and Neel and Weiss (1975).

Fecundity, fertility and child bearing have a number of related problems. The first is the foetal loss and pregnancy wastage, studies in which have been conducted by Bresler (1970) on white population in Caucasians, and Resseguie (1974) on Amish population. The second is the problem of still births and its effect on subsequent reproduction behaviour. This has been analysed by Alberman (1974) and Vogel and Knox (1975). The third and very important aspect is of the infant mortality and death syndrome. Some of the important examinations have been conducted by Vatwani (1973), Greenberg et al (1973), Spiers (1974), Franklin (1974), Singh (1974) and the annual global data is provided in the World Health Statistics Report (1974).

Studies on differential fertility have been carried out in 1970 by Hussain, in 1974 by Karim and King and in 1976 by Ram and Dutta and Gurumurthy. The demographic picture of Parsis of Karachi has been drawn by Gustafson (1969) and social and economic variations in child spacing has been discussed by Davidson (1970).

The socio-economic factors that determine the level of human fertility are exposure or non-exposure to pregnancy through marriage and separation. The exposure begins with marriage provided puberty was reached well before and provided the marriage takes place when the woman is fecund. The mean age at marriage is, therefore, a significant factor to study.

The female marriage age in India is very low and fertility is high (Agarwala, 1962). There has been a constant rising trend in this mean age; it has risen from 13.14 in 1911 to 15.8 in 1971. The difference in ages of husband and wife has decreased from an average of 7 years (1951) to 5.8 years in 1971. This increase in average age at marriage plays a positive role in reducing fertility as shown by various studies e.g., Chandrasekharan (1948), Sovani (1948), Wattal (1958), Balakrishna (1961), Mukherjee (1962), Berrai et al (1968), Bumpass (1969), Matsunaga and Tonomura (1972), Selvin and Garfinkel (1972, 1976), Matsunaga (1973),

Goyal (1975) as also Luella (1974) Mo-Im et al (1974) and Chauhan (1974). This phenomenon is caused by reduction in the reproductive span of the female and promotion of an attitude in the couple of fertility reduction. Agarwala (1970) has made calculations to find out the likely decline in birth rate in India as a result of female marriage age rising to 19-20 years and has estimated a reduction of 30% *in* the birth rate.

The effects of marital status on fertility of rural-urban and urban-rural migrants have been discussed by Ritchey (1973) and on the rural-urban differences in the distribution of birth orders by Veevers (1973). Similarly the relationship between income and fertility was explored on the basis of Census data for 1960 by Cho (1968). It was observed that while the traditional inverse relationship still existed among American negroes, it no longer held good in the case of white population. Studies on the ages at menarche and menopause have been conducted by Mamoria (1965), Bardhan (1966), Buck and Stavarky (1967), Khan (1973), Goyal (1974), Selvin and Garfinkel (1976) etc. Studies on the menarcheal age of 581 girls from the Romanian Black sea port were carried out by Stukovsky et al (1967). The inter-relation of season of birth, parental age, menarcheal age, and body form of young women was studied by Hillman et al (1970). A study of sexual maturation of Indian girls in Andhra Pradesh was carried out by Bai and Vijayalakshmi (1973). A comprehensive study of ages at menarche, menopause and intervening fecundibility has been conducted on 324 women after recording their menstrual histories by Treloar (1974).

The ages at menarche and menopause, according to Dandekar (1974), in general, in India are 13 and 45, respectively. This age span she has divided into four periods from 13 to 20, 21 to 26, 27 to 33 and 34 to 45. She has concluded that average number of 7 children born per woman not exercising any control on fertility are uniformly distributed over these 4 periods, taking into account primary and secondary sterility.

Nutrition, environment, socio-economic conditions and state of health are the chief factors affecting the ages of menarche and menopause and these in turn determine the respective reproductive span of a woman which is an important aspect of her fertility. The findings of Clegg and Harrison (1971), Baker and Dutt (1972), Abelson (1976) and Dutt (1980) show that at high altitude the stress of hypoxia acts to reduce fertility.

The level of education of husband and wife and their economic status also play important role in child bearing, as shown by various studies conducted in this field. Nayar (1974), Gupta et al (1975) and Frinsancho et al (1976) have reported negative correlation between the economic status and fertility. Chauhan (1974) is of the view that because higher education means higher age at marriage it is the latter rather than the former that reduces fertility. However, the study conducted in 1970 by De Camargo et al., shows that education plays a major role in the process of modernization and in the adoptation of modern family pattern. Women's educational attainment was found linked in an inverse way with fertility at Sao Paulo, Brazil. Attempts have also been made to study the effect of consanguineous marriages on fertility among north-Indian Muslims by Basu (1975) and among French population by Philippe (1974).

Another important area in the current topic is the role of morphological traits in fertility performance. Differential reproductive performance among members of a population is the ultimate mechanism affecting the dynamics of the fertility process. Differential fertility in relation to physique is liable to change, because body dimensions are susceptible to change under environmental and genetic stresses. The extent to which individual body dimensions are correlated to fertility is a matter of close examination. While within India there is little literature in this area, outside India there have been quite a few discussions (Davenport, 1923, Eaton and Mayer, 1953, Howells 1953, Clark and Spuhler, 1959, Damon and Nuttal, 1965, Damon and Thomas, 1967, Mitton, 1975; Vetta, 1975; Lasker and Thomas, 1976). It has been found that stockier American parents produce larger families than slender parents. As regards association between height and weight and fertility, Grants technique (1951) is a useful contribution. While Mueller (1979) has studied correlation of physique and fertility in a malnourished population, Bailey and Garn (1979) have analysed data relating to American females to show socio-economic interaction between physique and fertility.

THE PROBLEM OF STUDY

Thus among the various topics and aspects of study, the problem relating to fertility and the bio-social factors affecting it, have in the recent years attracted the attention of anthropologists. It has been recognised that socio-demographic background plays a vital role in fertility performance. This subject has gained added importance in view of the intense need felt to contain the fast and accelerated growth of the population with a view to providing the people with better standards of living.

However, from most of the studies on Indian population groups it is quite apparent that while there has to be a general national policy on the control of the population growth, different regions of the country may warrant different emphasis.

The present study has been conducted in Kashmir valley on Kashmiri Pandits and Kashmiri Muslims. The Kashmiri Pandits are considered to be purest descendants of the Indo-Aryan race. Kashmir was not only inhabited by these Hindus (called Pandits) but was also ruled by Hindu kings belonging to various dynasties up to the end of 13th century. For brief period towards the end, the reign passed into the hands of a Buddhist ruler Ranchan (known by Kashmiris as Rentan Shan) who under the influence of a Muslim Saint Bulbulshah embraced Islam. But the rule on his death passed again into the hands of his Hindu queen Kota Rani. The Muslim rule came to the valley in 1339 when Shah Mir usurped the throne from her. With this started the conversion of Hindus into Islam forced by the rulers like Sikandar and aided by the Sayyads of Hamadan. With the passage of time the valley became a Muslim majority area.

Thus the two population groups, the Kashmiri Pandits and the Kashmiri Muslims though at one time constituted ethnically one homogenous population came to differ from each other in faith and customs and had snapped the marital ties with each other. Each community forms a respective Medelian population with intermarrying sub-castes.

Also, in view of a big post 1947 exodus of the Kashmiri Pandits from Kashmir to important cities of North India, it was thought proper to carry out the study on a sample of this immigrant pandit population of Delhi, to guage the extent, if any, to which migration, intermingling with other communities in this cosmopolitan city, the expansion of the horizon of outlook as also the change in the environment might have affected the fertility behaviour of this community. Not that a large significant variation could be expected between the sample drawn from Kashmir and that taken from Delhi; for the effect, if any, could be discerned only in the second and subsequent generation of the migrants.

To make the study more meaningful, population samples of both the Kashmiri Pandits and the Kashmiri Muslims respectively have been drawn from Srinagar and Sopore to give representation both to urban and semi-urban populations.

Thus the objective of the present study is to investigate the inter-population variations as well as intra-population variations with respect to the bio-socio-demographic features of the Kashmiri pandits and the Kashmiri Muslims.

To find out the inter-population variations, pandits have been compared with Muslim of Srinagar as well as of Sopore.

For studying intra-population variations, the urban pandits have been compared with semi-urban pandits and the urban Muslims with semi-urban Muslims. This has been done in view of the fact that there has been hardly any comparative studies conducted about urban vis-a-vis semi-urban populations with respect to their bio-demographic features, despite the fact that semi-urbanization is fast increasing all over the country.

It is to be observed that out of a total population of 4,63,879 (Municipal area—4,03,413) 88·69% is the urban component (4,11,395) (1971 census) at Srinagar. Therefore, the urban sample has been taken from Srinagar (Figs. I and II). According to 1971 census the total population of Sopore was 12,7,823 and the rural and urban population was in the ratio of 78.33 : 26.67. The semi-urban sample is, therefore, taken from Sopore (Figs. I and II).

Also, a migrated urban Pandit population sample from Delhi (Fig I) has been compared with the urban pandits of Srinagar as well as with the semi-urban pandits af Sopore.

The bio-socio-demographic features studied include fertility, mortality, various biological and socio-economic factors affecting fertility and the growth rate in terms of increase in family size.

Another objective of the present study is to determine, in all the five population samples of Kashmiri Pandits and Muslims, the extent of birth control practices and the acceptance of family planning measures by women belonging to different socio-economic groups. Further, the differences between desired and actual behaviour regarding fertility and sex-ratio of the children among the users and non-users of birth control devices, have been estimated.

In the light of various studies done on the association between fertility and physique, an effort has been made to assess the effect of body constitution of mothers on their fertility and also to examine the relationship between physique of mothers and sex-ratio of their children in both the Kashmiri Pandits and Kashmiri Muslims.

Finally, an attempt has been made to make an interpopulation comparison of Kashmiri Pandit and Karhmiri Muslim women with respect to their body dimensions in high and low fertility groups.

THE PLACE

The state of Jammu and Kashmir has an area of 2,22,236 km^2 and a population of 46,17,000 (1971 census). The state comprises the following three main physical areas :

(*i*) The northern region beyond zogilla range of outer Himalayas drained by the middle reaches of the river Indus.

(*ii*) The valley of Kashmir lying between Himalayan ranges and drained by the Jhelum and Kishen Ganga rivers.

(*iii*) The southern strip of the Jammu plains drained by the upper reaches of the river Chenab (Tikkoo, 1979).

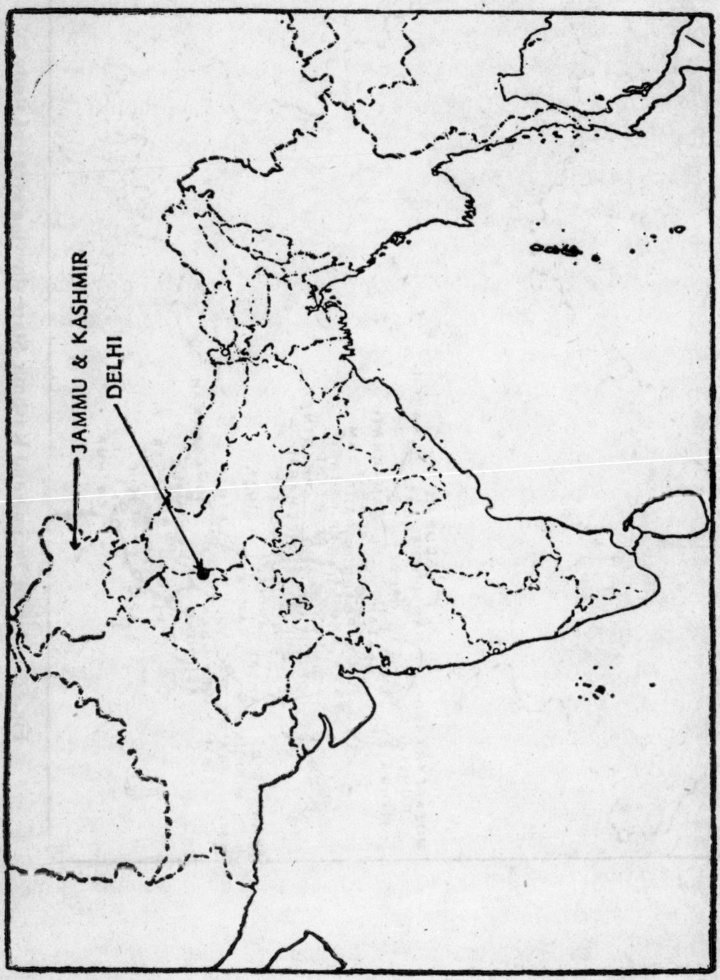

Fig. 1. Map of India showing areas of study.

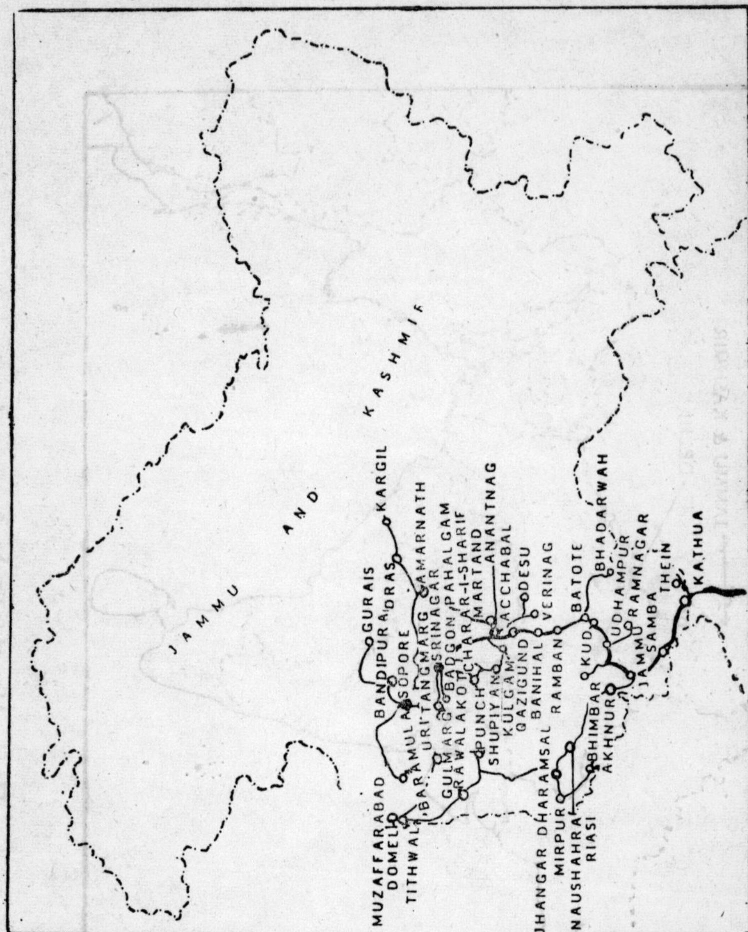

Fig. 2. Map of Jammu and Kashmir State showing areas of study.

Kashmir is the area inhabited by Kashmiris whose language is Kashmiri. This approximately corresponds to the ancient Kasmira-an irregularly oval valley 134 kms. long from North-East to South-West and 32 to 40 kms broad, between 33° to 34°35'N and 74°8' to 75°25' E. This picturesque valley is surrounded by mountain ranges varying from 12,000 to 18,000' in height. To the north lies a series of mountains which hasten away in wild confusion to the great promontory of Naga Parbat (26,182'). To the east rises Harmukh (16,903') which guards the valley of Sindh. On the South is Mahadeo hill looking down upon Srinagar, the high range of Gwash Brari (17,800') and the lofty peak of Amarnath (17,321'). The Pir-Pantsal range with peaks of 15,000' stands on the South-west. Further north is Tos maidan (14,000') and in the north-West, rises the majestic kajınag (12,125'). The place gets its name from a sage Kashyapa who is supposed to have founded it.

Neelamatpurana describes at length how Kashmir was created out of water and left to the care of the Nagas (Tikkoo, 1979). Kashmir, according to this work was "Sati Sar" (Sati lake) transformed into land. A water-demon named Jalodbhava was causing great trouble by killing the inhabitants of neighbouring regions. Neela went to his father Kasyapa and asked him to get rid of the wicked demon. At the request of Kasyapa, Vishnu slew him. Thereafter Kashmira came to be inhabited by human beings. That the place was founded by Kasyapa is corroborated by the fact that the foreign chronicler, Hecataeus refers to it as Kaspatyros. Hiuen Tsang has referred to it as Kia-Shi-mi-lo (Ray, 1957).

The name of Kasmira does not occur in the Vedic literature. In Sanskrit literature, the earliest reference to Kasmira is found in Panini's grammar and in Patanjali's great commentary on it. There the term Kasmira and its derivation Kaasmira are stated as the name of the country and its inhabitants, respectively. The Mahabharata also makes reference to Kashmiras. Ptolemy (150 A.D.) refers to the region as Kaspeira and Alberuni also has referred to Kashmira in his Kitab-ul-Hind (Ray, 1957).

A city by the name of Srinagri was originally built by Ashoka in the 3rd century B.C. In the 6th century A.D. Pravarasena II founded his capital Pravarapura adjacent to Srinagri. In due course of time this Parvarapura came to be known as Srinagar and the original city was given the name of Pandrethan (Puranadhistana), meaning old centre. The present Srinagar is situated on either banks of river Jehlum at 34° latitude and 75° longitude, approximately. The city has an area of 368 km² and its altitude is 1,768 metres. It gives shelters to a population of 4,63,879 people (1971 census). Majority of these are Muslims (3,45,141) only about 13% (52,172) (1971 census) are Hindus who are known as Kashmiri Pandits.

The semi-urban township of Sopore, selected for the present study, is situated about 35 kms. to the north-west of Srinagar city near the famous Wulur lake at approximately 74.2° longitude and 34.2° latitude. It has a population of 1,27,823 (27,697 in the town area). Majority of these are Muslims (25,630-1971 census) and only 1,961 are Kashmiri Pandits. This was one of the three towns built during the reign of king Avantivarman in 9th century A.D. The first was Avantipura built by the king himself, the second was Surapura built by his minister Sura and the third was Suryapura built by his Irrigation minister, Surya. Suryapura has become the modern Sopore (Ray, 1957).

Delhi is the capital of India. It has been the capital of so many rulers in the past and after independence it has got an added importance as the seat of the Union Government of Independent India. Over the years it has obtained a cosmopolitan character and sizeable population of Kashmiri Pandits has recently (since 1946-47) migrated from Kashmir and settled here too. The total population of Kashmiri pandits in Kashmir and outside Kashmir is less than one lakh (Kaul, 1978). However, there is a negligible population of Kashmiri Muslims as they migrate to Delhi and other cities in the plains only temporarily during winters for employment, trade and commerce, and hence they were not covered under this study.

THE PEOPLE

Kashmir valley closetted between mountain ranges has had a

chequered history because of which its population composition has undergone great many changes.

There are few sources which throw some light on the type and character of the caste system in vogue in ancient Kashmira. Early works like Nilamatapurana mention Brahmins distinctly as the upper most caste of the valley. According to Rajatarangini of Kalhana there were several low castes among the population viz., Nisadas, Kiratas, Kaivartas, Dombas, Svapakas and Chandalas (Ray, 1957).

From the remotest time up to the coming of the Islam people belonging to different ethnic groups, had come to Kasmira, settled in the valley and had gradually merged into homogenous Kashmiri people. That is why we find in the very formation of their bodies, in their language and in their culture, traces of different racial characteristics. In the 2nd century B.C. Sakas migrated to the valley from the neighbouring Baltistan. From the first to the fourth century A.D. Yue-chis, the stock to which the Kusanas belonged, settled here. Likewise, Hunas found shelter in this secluded valley during 5th and 6th century. Gujar emigration took place from North Punjab and that of Tibetans from Tibet. Considerable migrations of populations into the territory of Kasmira had taken place from Indian plains too, and the picture that emerges is of a race termed as Indo-Afghan by Haddon, as Nordic by Guha, or as Indid by Von Eickstedt (quoted from Ray, 1957). Kashmiri Pandits have been considered to be the descendants of the "Indo-Aryans" in the purest form by Guha (Ray, 1957). The majority of Kashmiri people possess a light transparent brown skin and usually of medium to tall stature. They are dolichocephalic, have a well-developed fore-head, a long narrow face, and a prominent straight and finely cut leptorrhine nose.

Damodar Gupta, Ksemendra, Bilhana, Mankha and the great Chronicler Kalhana give us an account of the period up to 12th century A. D. during which the valley was inhabited by Hindus only. The prominent dynasties that ruled included Gonandiya, Turuskas, Karkota, Utpals and Lohara (Tikkoo, 1979). Jonaraja carries the chronicle from the 12th century to early 15th century.

Accordingly, Muslim rule is said to have come to the valley around 1339 when Shah Mir usurped the throne from Kota Rani, the last Hindu ruler and adopted the title of Sultan Shamsud-din. Simultaneously, Islam spread in Kashmir through the Sayyeds from Hamadan who had fled from the city of Iran at the onslaught of Taimur and taken refuge in Kashmir. They aided and instigated Sikandar (1389-1413 A. D.) in destroying precious heritage of Kashmir embodied in treatises and cultural institution as also in forcible conversion of people. The tyrany of this sixth ruler of Shah Miri Sultans led to the first mass exodus of Pandits from Kashmir to other parts of the country. When Zain-ul-Abidin, the second son of Sikandar ascended the throne in 1420 A. D., he invited these Pandits to return and resettle in Kashmir. But after Zain-ul-Abidin, Kashmiri Brahmins again faced religious onslaught against them during the reign of Chaks (1530 to 1585), Mughals (1585 to 1852) and Pathans (1753 to 1819) with the result that sporadic exodus of Kashmiri Pandits from the valley to the plains of North India continued. After attaining Independence in 1947, Delhi became an attraction for the people from all corners of the land as it grew as a central seat of the Union Government. Kashmiri Pandits, who in comparison to their Muslim friends were more educated, came out of Kashmir for better educational and economic prospects and thus, in due course the second largest concentration of Kashmiri Pandits came into being at Delhi. During 1951-1961 there was a net loss of 56,000 due to migration from the State of Jammu and Kashmir as a whole (Vaidyanathan, 1967).

CHAPTER

2

Materials and Methods

METHODS OF SAMPLING

To AVOID any bias, the households were selected at random from various localities in Srinagar, Sopore and Delhi to give a representative population of these areas. For urban Kashmiri Pandits, samples were drawn from Habbakadal, Alikadal, Karan Nagar, Safakadal, Jawahar Nagar, Broadway and Rainawari clusters in Srinagar and Laxmibai Nagar, Shakti Nagar, Timarpur, Kidwai Nagar, Pamposh Enclave clusters in Delhi respectively.

For semi-urban Kashmiri Pandits, samples were drawn from the colony, Batapora and Ghanai mohala in Sopore.

For Kashmiri Muslims sampling were drawn from the Muslim clusters in the same areas in Srinagar and Sopore where the Kashmiri Pandit samples were drawn.

While no selection or distinction as such was made while collecting the sample, the closely related married women were avoided as for as possible. For this purpose, only one married woman was selected from each household.

These selected women from each household acted as our primary informants.

METHODS OF COLLECTING DATA

On the basis of a pilot study done earlier with the interview guide as a tool, an open ended questionnaire was developed for the survey.

The door to door survey was conducted using the open-ended questionnaire. Also, heavy reliance was placed on the Interview method. This involved indirect and non-formal conversations not only with the primary informants but also with the other members of her household.

Consequently, one did not have to rely entirely on the memory of the informant for recording vital data relating to marriage, births and more particularly ages.

Further, the questionnaire itself was designed in such a way so that answers to various questions were cross-checked to remove inconsistencies, if any. For instance, we have checked the off-hand reply of the subject regarding her age with four to five more answers as-age at marriage, duration of married life, age at first birth and age at the last birth.

The questionnaire included the questions pertaining to sex, age compositions, marital status, fertility, ages at marriage, menarche, menopause and each parity, use of birth control devices and attitude towards family size.

Besides, collecting bio-socio demographic information the following anthropometric measurements were also taken on the primary informant (ego) using standard techniques and precautions (Singh and Bhasin, 1968) in order to understand the impact of physique on the relative fertility of the Kashmiri Pandit and the Kashmiri Muslim women.

1. Height vertex
2. Body weight
3. Chest girth
4. Hip girth
5. Maximum calf girth
6. Maximum upper arm girth
7. Skinfold at bicep
8. Skinfold at tricep

The anthropometric measurements were taken on 107 unrelated Kashmiri Pandit women and 168 Kashmiri Muslim women from Srinagar and Sopore who (along with their husbands) have never used any birth control device.

METHODS OF ANALYSIS OF DATA

The intricate relationship between social values, beliefs and fertility has always concerned demographers. It has, therefore, been felt necessary to take every care to evaluate fertility performance of the Kashmiri Pandit and Muslim population samples from Srinagar, Sopore and Delhi with due regard to the limitation of the samples. Known mathematical formulae have, therefore, been adopted to arrive at the fertility rates. Since an electronic calculator has been used, there is a slight variation in the fractions in rounding off.

The demographic information collected about the Kashmiri Pandit and Muslim samples of Srinagar, Sopore and Delhi respectively, was treated in the following manner :

Age and Sex Composition

This gives an idea of the general population structure. Also, it serves to indicate number of individuals and the proportion of males in the reproductive age group i.e. an estimation of the size of breeding population which may cause variation in fertility behaviour.

Fertility rates have been measured according to the formulae given by Barclay (1958).

Child-Woman Ratio

This is the ratio of children in the age-interval of 0-4 years to per 1000 women of child-bearing age. The formula is P_{0-4}/F_{15-49}- $X\ K$, where P is the number of children below 5 years and f the number of females between 15-29 years of age and K is 1000.

Crude Birth Rate

This has been arrived at by dividing the number of birth during the year by the mid-year population and multiplying by 1000.

General Fertility Rate

It is obtained by dividing the number of live birth in the year by the number of women biologically able to bear a child and multiplying by 1000. For this purpose, mothers between the age of 15 and 49 years have been taken into acccount because it has been presumed that as a rule only a negligible number of women outside this age limit would give birth to children.

Age-specific Birth Rates

This rate is obtained by dividing the number of live births of mothers of each age by the number of women of that age, and then multiplying the diviser by 1000. The formula used is $B/P\ K$ where B is the number of live births during the year to women in the age interval and P is the mid-year population of women in the same age group and K is 1000.

In this method emphasis is laid on the specific time period to live births and women. Because of this the formula is considered to give accurate results.

Total Fertility Rate

It is the sum of age-specific birth rates of women at each age from 15 to 49 years (with intervals of 5 years). The result is multiplied by 5. The method is useful to summarise the frequency of births in a particular year.

Cummulative Natality Rate

This rate estimates the number of children an age-group of 1000 women would deliver from the time they began child-bearing until they reach a specific age, if they were exposed to the age-specific birth rates in effect at a given time. To make the calculation the age specific birth rate is multiplied by 5 of the next five year age group.

Gross Reproduction Rate

This shows how many-girl babies—potential future mothers—would be born to 1000 women passing through their Child bearing years, if the age specific birth rates of a given year remained constant and if no women entering the child bearing period died before reaching menopause (Thompson and Lewis, 1965).

This rate can be found out by multiplying total fertility by the percentage of all births that are female births.

The anthropometric information gathered about the Kashmiri Pandit and Kashmiri Muslim women of Srinagar and Sopore was treated in the following manner :

Ponderal Index : This has been computed to obtain an integrated assessment of the stature of the selected subjects by using the formula,

$$\text{Ponderal Index} = \frac{\text{Height}}{\sqrt[3]{\text{weight}}}$$

Muscle and Bone Content : This has been arrived at by the formula

$$D = d - \frac{S_1}{2} - \frac{S_2}{2}$$

where $d = \dfrac{c}{\pi}$

c = maximum girth of the upper arm

d = diameter of the upper arm

D = Muscle and Bone content

S_1 = Skinfold over tricep muscle

S_2 = Skinfold at tricep muscle

Statistical Formula Used

Simple percentages, averages, standard deviations and Standard error: These have been calculated whenever possible in order to gain insight into the distribution and quality of data.

Chi-square For differential fertility with social variables the chi-square test (x^2) as the test of significance have been used.

t-test and variance ratio tests (*F-test*) have also been used for understanding the level of significance for the differences in qualitative and quantitative characteristics, respectively.

The Sample

This study covered the Kashmiri Pandits living in Srinagar, (the urban sample), Sopore, (the semi-urban sample) and

Delhi (the urban migrant sample). It also covers the Kashmiri Muslims living in Srinagar (the urban sample) and Sopore (the semi-urban sample)—the migrant Muslim population being negligible was not studied.

The distribution of the number of households in each of the five Kashmiri Pandit and Muslim samples of Srinagar, Sopore and Delhi is given in the table 2.1.

Table 2.1

Distribution of the Kashmiri Pandit and the Muslim samples from Srinagar, Sopore and Delhi

Population samples	*No. of house-holds*	*Males*		*Females*		*Total*
		No.	*%*	*No.*	*%*	
Pandits						
Srinagar (P_{S_r})	185	948	54.1	804	45.9	1752
Sopore (P_{S_o})	122	467	52.8	418	47.2	885
Delhi (P_D)	99	281	53.6	243	46.4	524
Muslims						
Srinagar (M_{S_r})	185	1090	54.7	901	45.2	1991
Sopore (M_{S_o})	148	958	52.1	880	47.9	1838
Total						6990

185 households of Kashmiri Pandits and an equal number of Kashmiri Muslim households have been surveyed from Srinagar.

In Sopore, only 122 households of Kashmiri Pandits as against 148 households of Kashmiri Muslims have been covered. This is so because of the fact that Pandit population forms hardly 7% of the total population in Sopore (1971 census). In Delhi, 99 households of Kashmiri Pandits have been surveyed. In all 6990 Kashmiri individuals have been covered.

Further, it is observed that in each of the five Kashmiri Pandit and Muslim samples under study, the percentages of males are higher than those of females, revealing the masculine character of Kashmiri populations irrespective of whether they are Hindus (known as Pandits) or Muslims by faith and irrespective of whether they belong to urban or semi-urban areas.

Population Composition of the Kashmiri Pandit and Muslim samples from Srinagar, Sopore and Delhi

According to A.H. Hawley (1959), the basic reasons for the study of the composition of population are following:

1. Data on composition make possible an elaboration of the description of a population and therefore permit detailed inter-population comparisons.

2. These data describe the various essentials like age, sex, etc. for analysing demographic processes e.g. birth, death and migration. In the absence of direct information on demographic processes, composition data, especially age and sex data provide a means for estimating the incidence of birth and death.

Thus, the varying trends of fertility, mortality and migration affect the age and sex composition of a population to varying extents and together they give a particular shape and size to it. This is why age-structure of a population is dif̄erent from that of another both in time and space.

Sex Composition

The sex composition gives a comparative picture of the numerical dominance of the one sex over the other. The proportion of males to females in a population is expressed by sex ratios (Desai, 1969).

In this study, the sex-ratio has been estimated by dividing the total number of females by the total number of males and multiplying the result by 1000 (According to 1971 Indian Census).

In a population with an equal number of males and females, the sex-ratio is 1000, with more females than males it is over 1000 and with fewer females than males it is less than 1000.

According to Stern (1968). the sex-ratio at fertilization is called the primary sex-ratio, that at birth, the secondary sex-ratio and that at among mature adults, the tertiary sex-ratio.

There are two major mechanisms that can lead to variation in the primary and secondary sex ratio from the expected 1000. (Cavalli-Sforza and Bodmer 1972):

1. There may be deviation from 1000 in the sex-ratio of fertilized zygotes caused either by different rates of production of *X*- and *Y*-carrying sperms or by difference in the efficiency with which the two types of sperms effect fertilization.

2. There may be differential mortality of males and females after fertilization.

Variation in the tertiary sex-ratio from the expected 1000 is caused partly due to variation in the primary and secondary sex ratio and partly due to differential mortality rates of males and females leading to differential viability of males and females under similar health hazards.

Since the sex ratio varies with age, due to differential mortality of two sexes, the total sex-ratio of a population is among many other factors, a function of age distribution of the population (Cavalli-Sforza and Bodmer, 1972).

When over all sex-ratio of each of the five population samples under study is viewed, it is seen (table 2.2) that there is an excess of males over females, similar to that found in the total Indian population (sex ratio being 930-1971 census) and in the J & K state as a whole (sex ratio being 878-1971 census).

Further, it is observed that with a sex-ratio of 918, Kashmiri Muslims of Sopore are closest to the Indian population as a whole, while Kashmiri Pandits of Delhi (sex-ratio being 865) and Kashmiri Pandits of Sopore (sex-ratio being 895) are closer to J & K state population as a whole.

However, Kashmiri Pandits and Muslims of Srinagar show much lower sex-ratio than even J & K state as a whole, their sex-ratio being 848 and 827 respectively.

According to the universal experience, the surplus of males at

Table 2.2

Age-wise Sex-Ratio Among the Kashmiri Pandits and the Muslims

Age Groups (in years)	*Sex Ratio*				
	Pandits			*Muslims*	
	Srinagar	*Sopore*	*Delhi*	*Srinagar*	*Sopore*
0-4	916	952	500	726	761
5-9	918	964	909	1252	1326
10-14	865	932	632	842	984
15-19	823	813	1032	655	703
20-24	791	932	814	884	719
25-29	818	769	690	851	987
30-34	889	1040	909	938	1292
35-39	889	1000	1214	879	944
40-44	795	708	1278	810	878
45-49	784	762	1000	707	848
50-54	621	692	680	933	1227
55-59	737	778	800	607	571
60-64	824	1000	500	535	676
65+	810	909	1556	704	808
Total	848	895	865	827	918

birth is progressively diminished due to high mortality rate among males at every age level, until during a certain period the sex-ratio is 1000 and after this, the proportion of males goes on decreasing compared to the number of females (McKusick, 1972).

The figures [1 (a) and (b)] exhibiting the sex-ratio in the various age groups in all the Kashmiri Pandit and Muslim population samples of Srinagar, Sopore and Delhi do not seem to follow this universal pattern for most of the age groups. In the 0-4 years age group, however, all the population samples under study have below 1000 sex-ratio, indicating thereby a preponderance of males at birth, conforming to the universal experience.

Thus, the Kashmiri Pandits of Srinagar show a paucity of females right from the birth, the sex ratio never rising equal to or above 1000 and the Kashmiri Muslims of Srinagar show a preponderance of females in the 5-9 years age group (sex ratio being 1252), followed by an excess of males over females beginning from 10 years onwards.

There is a preponderance of males than females among the Kashmiri Pandits and the Kashmiri Muslims of Sopore from the 5 years of age to 29 years. In the age group 30-34 years, both population samples have a higher proportion of females than the males, the sex ratio exceeding that of 1000.

In rest of the age categories the semi-urban Pandit sample from Sopore has a preponderance of males over females except in the age group of 35-39 years and of 60-64 years, where the number of males is equal to that of females.

The semi-urban Muslim sample from Sopore also has more numbers of males than females in all but one age-group, in the 50-54 years where the females outnumber the males.

The Delhi sample of Kashmiri Pandit shows various ups and downs in the sex-ratio. Till the age of 15 years, there are more males than females. 15-19 years age group shows an excess of females over the males.

From 20 to 34 years of age the males outnumber the females. There is paucity of males in the next two age groups, with the sex-ratio exceeding that of 1000. In the 45-49 years age group the

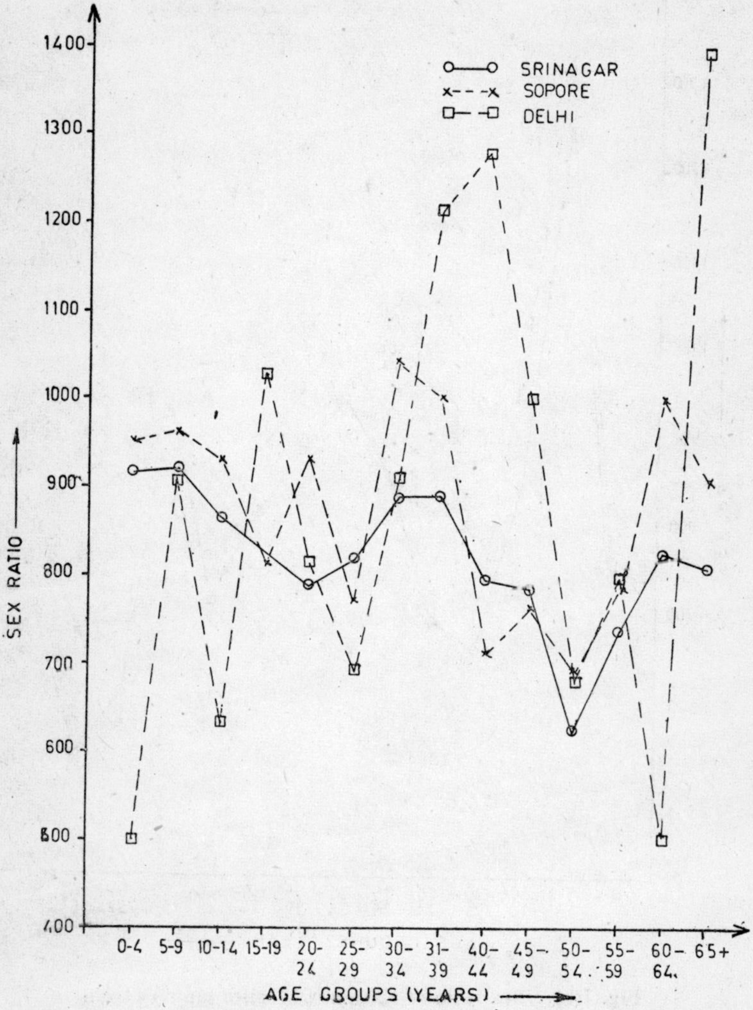

Fig. 1(a). Sex ratio of Kashmiri Pandit samples from Srinagar, Sopore and Delhi.

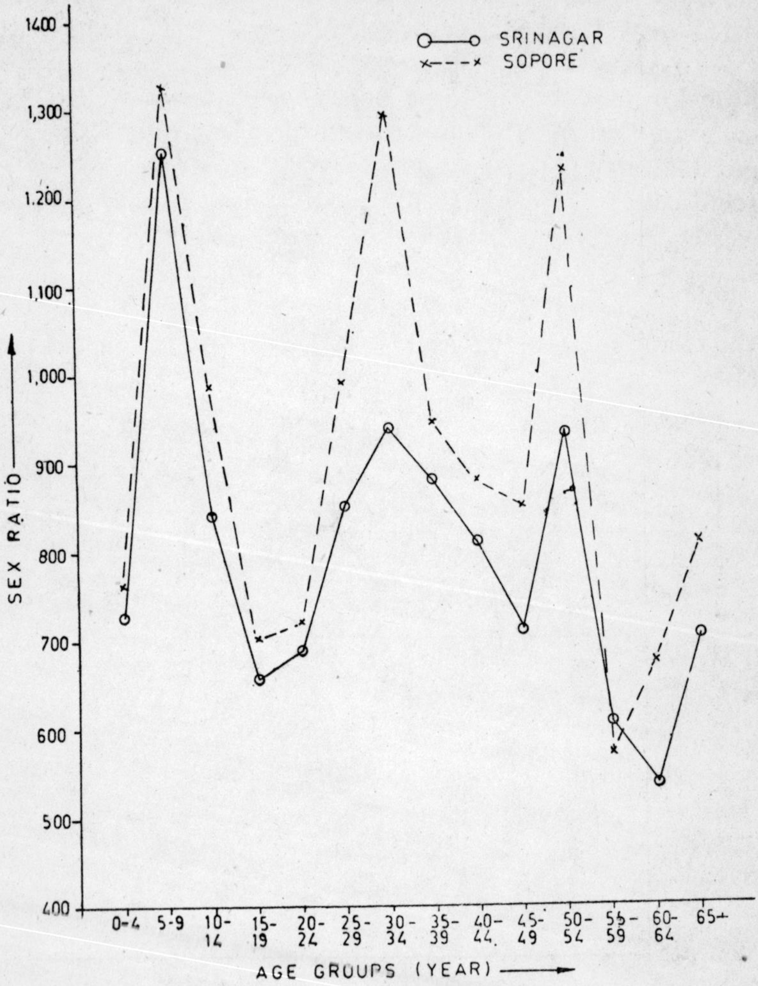

Fig. 1(b). Sex ratio of Kashmiri Muslim samples from Srinagar and Sopore

females are in as many numbers as the males. The next three age groups show a larger proportion of males than the females and in the above 65 years of age-group, females outnumber the males.

Thus it is found that among all the Kashmiri Pandit and Kashmiri Muslim sample of population under study, the Delhi sample of Kashmiri Pandits is the only population which shows a preponderance of females in the last age group, the 65+ years, conforming to the universal pattern and is an indicator of the greater longevity of females among the Kashmiri Pandits of Delhi.

Sex-ratio in the pre-fertile (0-14 years), fertile (15-49 years) and the post-fertile (50+ years) age groups are set out in table (2.3).

Table 2.3

Sex-Ratio in the Pre-fertile, Fertile & Post-fertile age groups among the Kashmiri Pandits and the Muslims

Population	*Sex-Ratio in the age-groups*		
	0-14 years	*15-49 years*	*50+years*
Pandits			
Srinagar	983	827	748
Sopore	1140	860	845
Delhi	680	991	884
Muslims			
Srinagar	940	789	695
Sopore	626	910	820

From the table and the figure (2) it is observed that in all the population samples under study, each broad age group (except 0-14 years in Pandits of Sopore) has a preponderance of males over females.

However, while the Pandits of Srinagar and Sopore and Muslims of Srinagar reveal a decrease in the proportion of females from the pre-child bearing age to child-bearing age, the Pandits of

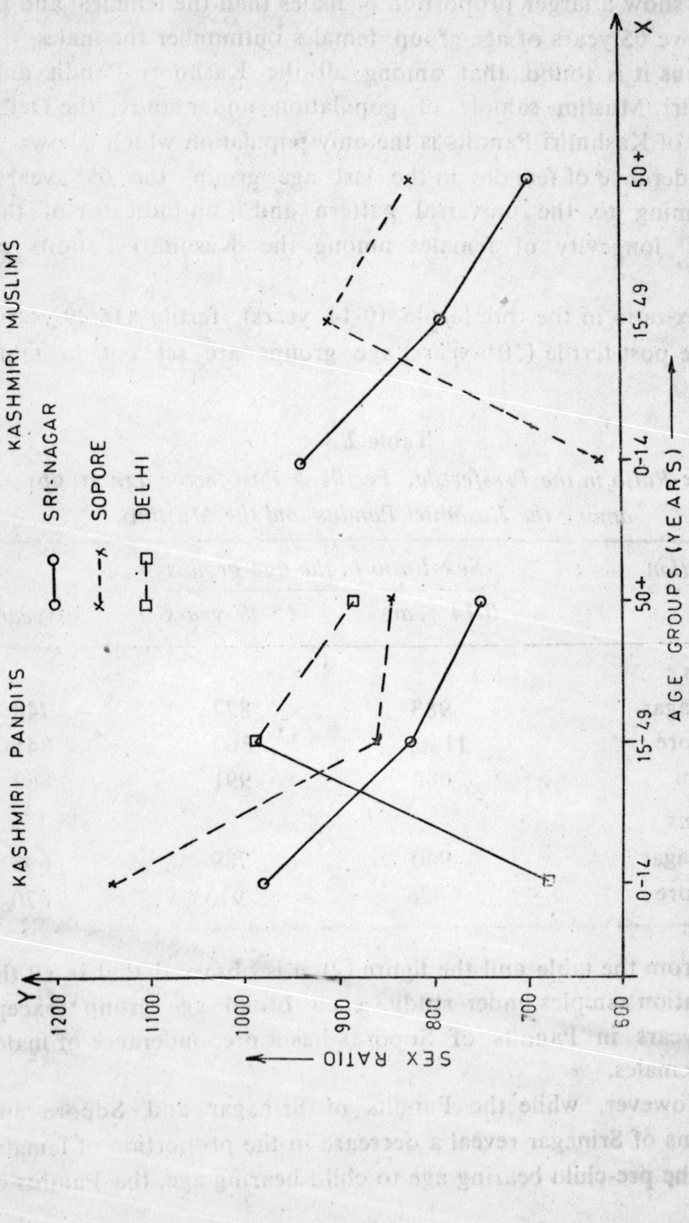

Fig. 2 Sex ratio in the pre-fertile, fertile and post-fertile age groups among the Kashmiri Pandits and Muslims

Delhi and Muslims of Sopore show an increase in the proportion of females in the reproductive age group from the proceeding age group which is bound to influence the relative population growth of the populations under consideration with the Pandits of Delhi and the Muslims of Sopore are at a greater risk of population growth but whether this materialises or not would depend upon a number of other important factors like the socio-economic condition and the degree of use of birth control measures.

In the post-child bearing age, the proportion of females is further reduced in all the population samples of Kashmiri Pandits and Muslims which indicates a higher post-reproductive female mortality in the Kashmiri population (Pandits and Muslims) as a whole.

Age Composition

The age composition of a population is much more complicated than its sex composition, because the ages in a population can be classified in a great number of ways. There is usually no confusion regarding the reporting of an individual's sex but errors can arise in reporting an individual's age because of ignorance or with the deliberate misreporting for some personal reasons.

Age distribution of a population implies how many persons there are at each age rather than the age of a population. The possibilities of errors in age-data are more when age classifications are based on single years and less when somewhat broader classes of age are used. The present data has been classified into 5 year categories.

It is apparent from the table (2.4) and figures [3 (a) & (b)] that in all the Kashmiri Pandit and Muslim population samples under study (except in the Delhi sample of Kashmiri Pandits), the higher percentage of population seems to belong to the age group 5-9 years rather than to the 0-4 years age-group.

This is against the universal experience as observed in other populations according to which 0-4 years age group has been found to include maximum percentage of a population because this represents the nearest to the original stock which compared with

Table 2.4

Age wise distribution of the Kashmiri Pandits and the Muslims

Age Group	Srinagar				Delhi		Sopore			
	Kashmiri Pandits		Kashmiri Muslims		Kashmiri Pandits		Kashmiri Pandits		Kashmiri Muslims	
	No.	%	No.	%	No.	%	No.	%	No.	%
0-4	159	9.08	252	12.66	24	4.58	82	9.27	243	13.22
5-9	305	17.41	313	15.72	21	4.01	163	18.42	300	16.32
10-14	304	17.35	280	14.06	31	5.92	141	15.93	248	13.49
15-19	175	9.99	182	9.14	63	12.02	87	9.83	172	9.36
20-24	154	8.79	165	8.29	78	14.89	85	9.60	153	8.32
25-29	140	7.99	161	8.09	49	9.35	69	7.80	155	8.43
30-34	102	5.82	62	3.11	21	4.01	51	5.76	55	2.99
35-39	119	6.79	186	9.34	31	5.92	54	6.10	173	9.41
40-44	79	4.51	105	5.27	41	7 82	41	4.63	92	5.01
45-49	66	3.77	70	3.52	52	9.92	37	4.18	61	3.32
50-54	47	2.68	58	2.91	42	8.02	22	2.49	49	2.67
55-59	33	1.88	45	2.26	27	5.15	16	1.81	33	1.80
60-64	31	1.77	66	3.31	21	4.01	16	1.81	57	3.10
65+	38	2.17	46	2.31	23	4.39	21	2.37	47	2.56
Total	1752		1991		524		885		1838	

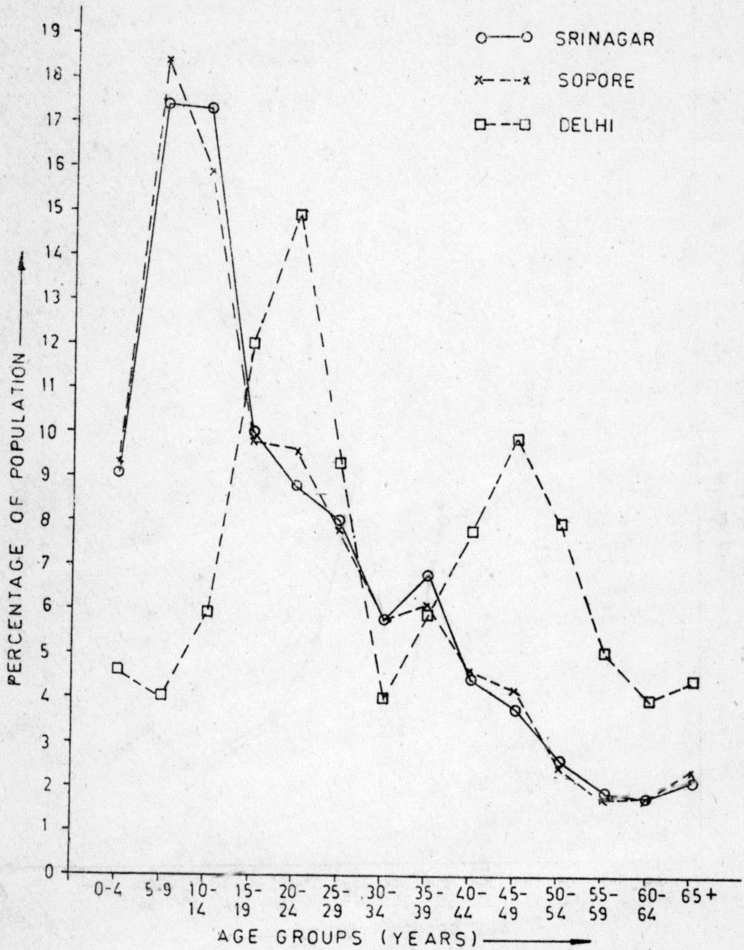

Fig 3(a) Age Distribution of the Kashmiri Pandit samples from Srinagar, Sopore and Delhi

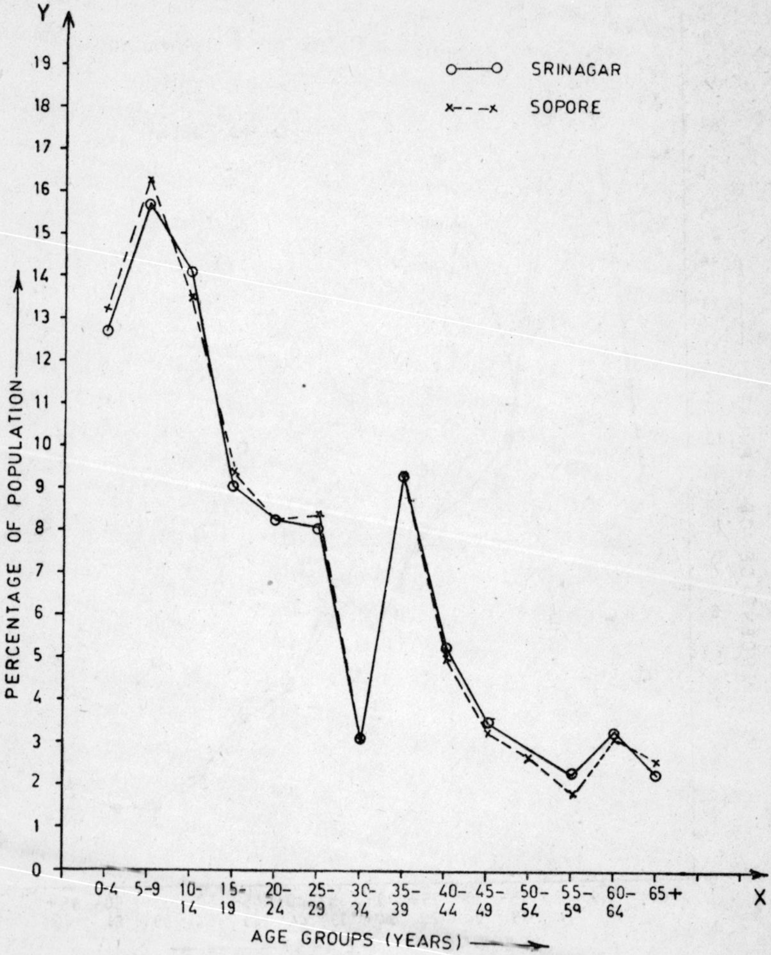

Fig 3(b) Age distribution of the Kashmiri Muslim samples from Srinagar and Sopore

other groups has been exposed to the minimum risks of death. The All India figures (1971 census) and the Jammu and Kashmir State as a whole (1971 census) also show the similar trend.

This anomaly may be either due to high fertility rate during the period 5-9 years age and/or high mortality rate in the 0-4 years age-group or it may be due to the impact of family planning measures as this is the most recent age-group of children as discussed later.

It is observed that the maximum decrease in the percentage population from 5-9 years to 0-4 years age-group has been among the Kashmiri Pandits of Srinagar (8.38) and Sopore (9.15) followed by Kashmiri Muslims of Sopore (3.10) and Srinagar (3.06). The Kashmiri Pandits of Delhi, however, show a slight increase of 0.57 from 5-9 years age group to 0-4 years because of better medical facilities in recent times available at Delhi. Besides a general better economic status of Kashmiri Pandits in Delhi which would have led to much better infant care and consequent reduction in infant mortality.

It seems that the impact of high fertility (in the period of 5-9 years age), high mortality and that of family planning measures (0-4 years period of time) is greatest among the Kashmiri Pandits of Srinagar and Sopore, followed by that of Kashmiri Muslims of Sopore and Srinagar and least in the Kashmiri Pandits of Delhi.

In all the Kashmiri Pandit and Muslim population samples (excepts in the Delhi sample of Kashmiri Pandits) the maximum percentage of total population falls in the age category 5-9 years.

Thereafter all of them show a slight decrease (around 2%) in the percentage population from 5-9 years to 10-14 years age group and then a steep fall in the percentage population (about 6%, slightly less in the Kashmiri Muslim sample of Sopore =4.13%). This steep fall indicates that the highest mortality could have occurred in the age group of 15-19 years in the Kashmiri Pandit and Muslim sample of Srinagar and Sopore respectively.

In the Kashmiri Pandit sample of Delhi, the maximum percentage to total population falls in the age category 20-24 and then there is a gradual fall in the percentage till the age group

30-40 years. This is followed by a gradual increase till the age-group 45-49 years followed by a decline almost till the last age group.

In the Kashmiri Pandit samples of Srinagar and Sopore, respectively, the decline in the percentage of population follows a slightly zig-zag but gradual route from the age of 10 years to above 65 years of age, which is quite similar to the trend observed in the All India population and in the J & K population, respectively, during 1971 census.

The decline in the percentage of population of Kashmiri Muslims of Srinagar and Sopore is also gradual till the age group 25-29 years, which is followed by a decrease in the next age group 30-34 years and again an increase in the age-group 35-39 years followed by a gradual decline till the last age-group.

Thus, the following features emerge from the age distribution of the Kashmiri Pandit and Muslim samples from Srinagar, Sopore and Delhi—It may be inferred that the population size has started shrinking for the last 20 years among the Kashmiri Pandits of Delhi (20-24 years age-group having the maximum population percentage), while among the rest of the Kashmiri Pandit and Muslim populations belonging to both Srinagar and Sopore, respectively, the population size has started shrinking only for the last ten years (maximum population percentage being in the 5-9 years age group).

The Pandits of Delhi have the lowest population percentage in the age-group 0-4 years (4.58), followed by the Pandits of Srinagar (9.08) and Sopore (9.27) and the highest in the Muslims of Srinagar (12.66) and Sopore (13.22).

It, thus, appears that the maximum impact of various socio-economic factors, including family planning, on fertility has been in the Delhi sample of Kashmiri Pandits, followed by the Kashmiri Pandits of Srinagar and Sopore and least in the Muslims of Srinagar and Sopore.

"Young", "Mature" and "Aged" Populations and Life Expectancy

The populations have been conventionally defined as "young"

if there are less than 4% of persons above the age of 64, as "mature" when this percentage is between 4% and 7% and as aged when it exceeds 7% (Badgaiyan, 1957).

This concept of "young", "mature" and "aged" populations when applied to these five Kashmiri Pandit and Muslim population samples under study, reveals that the Kashmiri Pandits and Muslims of Srinagar and Kashmiri Pandits and Muslims of Sopore are young populations with 2.17, 2.31, 2.37, 2 56 percentage of population above 64 years of age respectively.

But the Kashmiri Pandits of Delhi have 4.39% of the population over 64 years of age and is therefore categorised as "mature".

However, it may be inferred from these figures that among all the Kashmiri Pandit and Muslim samples, life expectancy is highest in the Pandits of Delhi and least in the Kashmiri Pandits of Srinagar. Rest of the population samples hold the intermediary positions.

Median Age of Populations and Life Expectancy

The only way in which a single age can be given for a group of persons is by using some sort of average. The age distribution of a population is very simply and most commonly described by its median age i.e., the age which divides a population into two equal halves, half above the median age and half below it.

A young population then is one that contains a large proportion of young persons and has a low median age, while an old population has a high median age and a large proportion of old people (Coale, 1972).

While Kashmiri Pandits and Kashmiri Muslims of Srinagar and Sopore, respectively, have an almost 10 years lower (see table 2.5) median age than the Kashmiri Pandits of Delhi. Again indicating much higher life expectancy of Delhi Pandits compared to any other population under study, which may be directly the result of better socio-economic* and medical conditions prevailing for the

*See Dependency Ratio.

Table 2.5

Median Age of the Kashmiri Pandit and the Muslim populations from Srinagar, Sopore and Delhi

Population	Median Age (in year)
Pandits	
Srinagar	22.3
Sopore	22.3
Delhi	32.9
Muslims	
Srinagar	23.3
Sopore	22.9

Kashmiri Pandits of Delhi than for other populations under study.

Whether a population is young or old depends upon its relative fertility and mortality. The declining birth and death rates are expected to increase the median age of a population. While rising birth and death rates are likely to cause a decline in the median age.

Dependency Ratio

Another more useful but complex way of describing the age-distribution of a population is dependency ratio. It is a measure of impact of age-composition on the economy (Jones, 1974; Shryock et al. 1971).

It is based on the fact that all the members of a population are consumers but that only some members are producers. For the international comparison, it is recognized that those under 15 are the dependent youth and those over 60 are dependent aged. The age-group 15-59 years is considered economically active part of population and is used as the base for calculating the dependency ratio (Thompson and Lewis, 1965).

The youth dependency ratio is calculated by dividing the number of people under 15 by the number of people aged 15-59 and multiplying the resulting qotient by 100. It has been found to be highest in the Kashmiri Pandits of Srinagar (83.93) and Sopore (83.55) followed by Kashmiri Muslims of Sopore (83.9) and

Srinagar (81.72) and it is drastically least in the Kashmiri Pandits of Delhi (18.81).

Similarly, the aged dependency ratio is calculated by dividing the number of those aged 60 years and above by number of those aged 15-59 years and multiplying the quotient by 100. It is found to be highest in the Kashmiri Muslims of Sopore (11.03) followed by Pandits of Delhi (10.9), Muslims of Srinagar (10.8), Pandits of Sopore (8.0) and least in the Pandits of Srinagar (7.54).

While youth dependency ratio and the median age of the populations are negatively associated with one another, the aged dependency ratio is positively correlated with the median age of the population (Thompson and Lewis, 1965).

A total dependency ratio is simply the sum of the youth dependency ratio and the aged dependeucy ratio.

Kashmiri Muslims of Sopore are found to have the highest total dependency ratio (94.91) followed by Kashmiri Muslims of Srinagar (92.5) Kashmiri Pandits of Sopore (91.6) Kashmiri Pandits of Srinagar (91.5) and least in the Kashmiri Pandits of Delhi (29.7).

Therefore, the Kashmiri Pandits and Muslims of Srinagar and Sopore are more under economic stress than the population of India as a whole, Dependency Ratio being 78 (Jones, 74). The reverse is true that of Pandits of Delhi.

This is a clear indication of Delhi Pandits being much better off than the Kashmiri Pandits of Srinagar and Sopore respectively, while the Kashmiri Pandits of Srinagar and Sopore seem to be only marginally economically better than the Kashmiri Muslims of respective areas.

Marriage-wise distribution of the Kashmiri Pandits and the Muslims

Consanguineous marriages are strictly prohibited in the Pandits while in the Muslims, such marriages with close relatives are preferred.

Results of the marriage-wise distribution of all the population samples of Kashmiri Pandits and Muslims have been set out in table 2.6.

Table 2.6

Marriage wise distribution of the Kashmiri Pandits and the Muslims

Type of marriage	*Population Samples*									
	Pandits						*Muslims*			
	Srinagar		*Sopore*		*Delhi*		*Srinagar*		*Sopore*	
	No.	*%*	*No.*	*%*	*No.*	*%*	*No.*	*%*	*No.*	*%*
parallel cousin	—	—	—	—	—	—	8	4.32	29	19.59
Cross-cousin	—	—	—	—	—	—	13	7.03	8	5.40
Other relations	—	—	—	—	—	—	18	9.73	24	16.22
No relation	165	100	122	100	99	100	146	78.92	87	58.78
Total	165	100	122	100	99	100	185	100.00	148	100.00

It is observed that as expected among the Pandit population samples from Srinagar, Sopore and Delhi, there is no marriage between the blood relations.

On the contrary, the Muslims of Srinagar show about 21% marriages between close blood relations. The frequency of consanguineous marriages among the semi-urban muslims is found to be almost double (41%) than that of the urban muslims of Srinagar.

Genetically, it is expected that the highest frequency of malformed children and of infant mortality may be among the semi-urban muslims, followed by urban muslims and least among the urban and semi-urban Pandits, on account of consanguineous marriages.

Since the Muslim population of Kashmir is only about thirty generations old, the selection-relaxation vis-a-vis incompatability effects may not be of significant consequence.

Family Typewise distribution of the Kashmiri Pandits and the Muslims

Traditionally, Kashmiri Pandits lived in joint families while Kashmiri Muslims lived in joint as well as in nuclear families. But the joint family system is fast breaking up due to the ever-rising costs of living and progressive erosion of middle class values.

It must be mentioned here that a family of husband, wife and unmarried children of them was considered to be nuclear as compared to the one in which one or more than one, other relatives were also living with them, considered as joint family.

Table 2.7

Family Type-wise distribution of the Kashmiri Pandits and the Muslims

Population	*Type of family*				*Total*
	Nuclear		*Joint*		
	No.	*%*	*No.*	*%*	
Pandits					
Srinagar	78	42.2	107	57.8	185
Sopore	67	54.9	55	45.1	122
Delhi	67	67.7	32	32.3	99
Muslims					
Srinagar	98	53.0	87	47.0	185
Sopore	53	35.8	95	64.2	148

From table (2.7), it is observed that among the Kashmiri Muslims, the percentage of joint families is higher in the semi-urban sample than in the urban sample.

However, among the Pandits, the highest frequency of joint families is in the urban sample from Srinagar, followed by semi-urban sample and least in the urban sample from Delhi.

The fact that the frequency of joint families in the semi-urban Pandits is about 13% less than in the urban Pandits, may be because of economic constraints that more of educated Pandits have moved out to cities.

Table 2.8

Education-wise distribution of the Kashmiri Pandits and the Muslims

Population	*Educational group*	*Husbands* No.	*Husbands* %	*Wives* No.	*Wives* %
Pandits					
Srinagar	(1) No formal education	—	—	36	19.46
	(2) Middle school	—	—	30	16.22
	(3) Secondary School	78	42.16	56	30.27
	(4) Graduation	72	38.92	46	24.86
	(5) Post-graduation & above	35	18.92	17	9.19
		185			
Sopore	(1) No formal educatian	4	3.28	55	45.08
	(2) Middle School	2	1.64	14	11.48
	(3) Secondary School	51	41.80	31	25.41
	(4) Graduation	46	37.70	19	15.57
	(5) Post-graduation & above	19	15.57	3	2.46
		122			
Delhi	(1) No formal education	—	—	24	24.24
	(2) Middle School	—	—	15	15.15
	(3) Secondary School	6	6.06	26	26.26
	(4) Graduation	36	36.36	22	22.22
	(5) Post-graduation & above	76	57.57	12	12.12
		99			
Muslims					
Srinagar	(1) No formal education	81	43.78	124	67.02
	(2) Middle School	16	8.65	28	15.14
	(3) Secondary School	55	29.73	15	8.11
	(4) Graduation	18	9.73	3	1.62
	(5) Post-graduation & above	15	8.11	15	8.11
		185			
Sopore	(1) No formal education	64	43.24	115	77.70
	(2) Middle School	12	8.11	1	6.76
	(3) Secondary School	35	34.65	1	10.14
	(4) Graduation	25	16.39	9	4.05
	(5) Post-graduation & above	12	8.11	2	1.35
		148			

Table (2.8) reveals that in case of husbands, the maximum percentage of them falls in the "Secondary level" among the Pandits of Srinagar and Sopore, in the "Post-graduation and above level" among the Pandits of Delhi and in the "no formal education level" among the Muslim population samples from Srinagar and Sopore.

However, in case of wives, the maximum percentage of them falls in the "Secondary level" among the Pandits of Srinagar and Delhi, in the "no formal education level" among the Pandits and Muslims of Sopore and Muslims of Srinagar.

Economic status-wise distribution of the Kashmiri Pandits and the Muslims

In order to assess the economic status of any population, it is necessary to know the annual per capita income of the household rather than the total income of the household. This is because, a household having high income but also having more economically inactive persons, the average gross expenditure on each member would be less than in a household having comparatively low income but also having fewer economically inactive members. So, the level of economic development of the household is measured as the annual per capita income.

On the basis of the median per capita income arbitrary economic classes have been identified in each population. These classes being :

1. Below median class
2. Median class
3. Above median class.

Table 2.9 reveals that the median per capita income of Delhi Pandits is comparatively much higher than those of other Pandit and Muslim population samples of Srinagar and Sopore.

It is observed that in all the Kashmiri Pandit and Muslim population samples of Srinagar, Sopore and Delhi (except the Kashmiri Pandit of Sopore), maximum percentage of the popula-

Table 2.9

Income-wise distribution of the Kashmiri Pandits and the Muslims

Population	*Annual per capita income of the household*		
	Below Median category	*Median category*	*Above Median category*
Pandits			
Srinagar	0-1500	1500-2000	2000+
Sopore	0-1500	1500-1800	1800+
Delhi	0-3600	3600-3850	3850+
Muslims			
Srinagar	0-2000	2000-2600	2600+
Sopore	0-1600	1600-1900	1900+

	No. of households in the						*Total*
	Below Median category		*Median category*		*Above Median category*		
	No.	*%*	*No.*	*%*	*No.*	*%*	
Pandits							
Srinagar	69	37.3	32	17.3	84	45.4	185
Sopore	53	43.4	21	17.2	48	39.3	122
Delhi	40	40.4	16	16.2	43	43.4	99
Muslims							
Srinagar	64	34.6	23	12.4	98	53.0	185
Sopore	46	31.1	37	25.0	65	43.9	148

tion belongs to above median category and least in the median category. In Kashmiri Pandits of Sopore, maximum percentage of the population belongs to below median category.

CHAPTER

3

Birth Control

The rapid increase in world population its outpacing the production and more particularly the food supplies is a sure threat to the mankind. In India particularly the growing population is the main cause of poverty, unemployment and the like. It is, therefore, natural that a family planning programme to arrest this growth should have attracted the attention of the authorities. An individual effort was made by Dr. Karve when he opened a family planning clinic in Bombay in 1925. At official level it was the Government of Mysore which stated a clinic in 1930, and was followed in 1932 by the Government of Madras. After independence, in 1949 a Family Planning Institute was set up in Bombay and in the same year the matter was discussed in the Planning Commission meeting. Since then this subject has gained such an importance that the allocation of expenditure has increased from a meagre Rs. 65.00 lakhs in the first five year plan to Rs. 5,160 lakhs in the fifth plan.

The guidelines giver by Freymann (1980) help in understanding the attitudes of the peoples towards the acceptance of family planning. He has categorised the family planning research into four groups: (*a*) population problem and the indentification of social variables can be made by broad demographic analysis, (*b*) the understanding of the individual biological unit can be arrived at on the basis of the investigation of the physiology of reproduction, (*c*) to devise various methods for birth control and (*d*) the habit of adopting new contraceptive practices.

The desire to strike a balance between the economic inputs and the number to be fed has given rise to scientific studies in the direction of family planning programmes the world over. Stoeckel and Choudhury (1969) have conducted studies in Bangladesh and Wright (1975) in the United States. Williamson (1980) has discussed the means of utilising the research to manage a family planning project. Raina (1969) has studied family size norms. Other important studies on the attitude to family size and sex preferences are those of Novitski and Kimball (1958), Pareek and Kothandapni (1969) Gustuvus and Nam (1970), Cutright et al (1974), Stinner and Mader (1975), Talwar (1975) and Coombs (1979).

There are 5132 main centres of family planning in rurul India with 33,370 sub-centres and 1975 centres in urban areas. It is estimated that during 1961-1975 as many as 20,5866 million births were averted with the help of sterilization, I.U.D.* and other family planning devices. By March 1980, the percentage of couples protected by these devices had risen to 22.6 (Srikantam and Saxena, 1981).

The various devices of family planning adopted in India are discussed below :

1. **I.U.D.*** It is estimated that by 1970 about 31 lakhs women had got loop inserted. This figure rose to 54.37 lakhs by 1975. A factory has been set up at Kanpur to manufacture loops. The service to insert loops is offered through mobile and static units. According to Annual Report 1979-80 Ministry of Health, 303,190 I.U.D. insertions have been done during 1979-80 (April to October, 1979).

2. **Sterilisation :** This is the most certain method of preventing pregnancy. In case of male this is known as vasectomy and in the case of females tubectomy or salpingectomy. It was estimated that in 1979-80 3,049,050 persons will get sterilised in India.

*Intra-uterine device.

There were initial reservations for this method but with proper education through clinics and Block Development Centres, these are being come over and the sterilisation is gaining popularity. By October, 1979 47.3% of this target was achieved.

3. **Contraceptives:** These include diaphragm for woman, condom for man, foam tablets, gellies, douche etc. Of these the condom popularly known as Nirodh is most commonly used in India. It is estimated that in 1979-80 (April to Sept., 1979) 92.55 million couples have taken to contraceptives. Nirodh is being distributed free of charge through various schemes as well as retailers.

4. **Oral contraceptive** : These are the tablets taken by women to avoid pregnancy. The scheme for distribution of oral tablets was introduced in India in 1967 and in 1979-80 (April to Sept., 1979) an estimated .80 lakh women have taken to the pill.

5. **Abortion** : Known technically as medical termination of pregnancy. An act dealing with this came into force in April 1972. It provides for termination of pregnancy by qualified doctors under specified circumstances. Various institutions numbering 1249 had been approved for this purpose by 1975 and 1.64 lakhs terminations had been registered. In 1979-80 (April to Sept., 79), 1.47 lakhs of terminations have been done.

In 1969-70 a post-partinum programme was started in 59 selected centres which has gone up to 255 by 1975. Under this scheme family planning is propagated among women attending hospitals for delivery.

In addition there are other methods like rhythm method. coitus-interruptus etc. which are not used in India widely but couples using these are found in the samples selected for study.

The present day problem therefore, is not one of non-availability or lack of knowledge of various methods of family planning but of motivating and educating people with a view to changing their attitudes towards accepting the idea of limiting their families.

Table 3.1 shows that both the users of Birth Control Devices (BCD) and Non-users of BCD among Kashmiri Pandits and Muslims of urban and semi-urban areas regard less than '3' as the desired number of children. The only exception is Muslims of

Table 3.1

(*Desired and Actual No. of children per couple among the Kashmiri Pandits and the Muslims*)

Population	*Contraceptive habits BCD users/ Non-users*	*No. of women*	*No. of children desired*			*Per couple actual*			*% increase over the desired No. of children*
			M	*F*	*T*	*M*	*F*	*T*	
Pandits									
Srinagar	Non users	51	1.69	1.05	2.71	1.77	1.28	3.05	11.31
	Users	134	1.68	1.02	2.70	1.28	1.19	2.47	8.52
	Total	185			2.71			9.63	
Sopore	Non users	89	1.71	1.21	2.99	1.86	1.26	3.12	4.35
	Users	33	1.56	1.22	2.78	1.37	1.42	2.79	0.36
	Total	122			2.93			3.03	
Delhi	Non users	19	1.45	1.21	2.66	2.33	1.62	3.85	44.74
	Users	80	1.32	1.27	2.59	1.35	1.47	2.82	8.88
	Total	99			2.60			3.02	
Muslims									
Srinagar	Non users	98	1.57	1.33	2.90	2.23	1.75	3.98	37.24
	Users	87	1.61	1.3	2.91	1.45	1.57	3.02	3.78
	Total	185			2.90			3.53	
Sopore	Non user	129	1.99	1.23	3.22	1.99	1.70	3.69	14.60
	user	19	1.72	1.27	2.99	1.35	1.72	3.07	2.68
	Total	148			3.19			3.40	

Sopore for whom desired number of children is a little more than '3'. Here it is interesting to recall the much publicised national slogan appealing to people to have 2 or 3 children only and no more. In all likelihood the national slogan appears to have made its desired impact on the Kashmiri populations.

Another obvious point to be taken into account is that when people speak of desired number of children they have survivors only in mind and not the number born.

Keeping these limitations in view we find that in all the population samples under study the non-users of birth control devices have exceeded the desired number of children by a large percentage than the users.

Looking into the desired number of children and the number of chi dren already among the users of birth control devices, it is seen that excepting the Pandits of Srinagar in whom the observed number of children is less than the desired number of children, in all other population samples under study, the observed number of children on an average is higher than the desired number. It, therefore, appears that the impact of national family planning slogans and programmes is realised profitably only among the Kashmiri Pandits of Srinagar while among the Kashmiri Pandits of Delhi and Sopore and Muslims of Srinagar and Sopore, respectively, the impact of national family planning programmes is yet to be realised.

The average number of children desired and the average number of children actually had by the couples in the samples belonging to different populations under study are set out in table (3.1) for the users of birth control devices (users of b.c.d.) and the non-users of birth control devices (non-users of b.c.d.) respectively. These values have been compared in order to understand the voluntary and the involuntary effects on the realisation of the desired number of children by the couple.

As already evidenced from table (3.1) the involuntary effect (as judged from the values for the non-users) is totally lacking. All the population samples have much higher average number of children than desired by the respective couples. Though this deviation is least and comparatively smaller among the Kashmiri Pandits of Sopore (4.35%) and maximum and rather very high among the Kashmiri Pandits of Delhi (44.74), such deviation is quite expected.

In the case where the voluntary control over the number of children is exercised, the differences between the desired and the observed number of children has been considerably brought down. Excepting the Kashmiri Pandits of Delhi in whom the average number of the observed children is about 9% higher than the average number of desired children, in no other populations the differences is more than +4%. The Kashmiri Pandits of Srinagar even show about 8.5% lower average number of observed childern than the average number of desired children.

Relatively, speaking the impact of Birth Control programmes among the users of birth control devices as measured in terms of the difference between the desired and the observed number of children, seems to be attained the most amongst the Kashmiri Pandits of Srinagar and the least among the Kashmiri Pandits of Delhi, while the Kashmiri Muslims of Sopore occupy the intermediary positions in this respect.

Estimation of success of Birth Control Devices and of Family Planning Programme among the Kashmiri Pandits and the Muslims.

From the present data, the impact of family planning programme can be measured for the different populations under consideration using the difference between the average desired number of children and the average observed number of children. While a positive difference will be an indicator of the lack of impact, a zero or a near zero difference will show the signs of success of family Planning measures. However, a negative difference will be a sure test of the use of Birth control devices in the desired direction (reduction in the family size).

These differences are set out in table (3.2) for the respective populations. Each population being split into the two categories of of (1) b.c.d. users and (2) b.c.d. non-users.

This difference is found to be positive in all the populations

Table 3.2

Estimation of success of birth control devices among the Kashmiri Pandits and the Muslims

Population	Users			Non-users			
	Proportion of b.c.d. user couples in the population	Difference between average of desired and observed no. of children	Weighted differences	Proportion of b.c.d. Non user couples in the population	Difference between average of desired and observed no. of children	Weighted difference	Total weighted difference between average of desired and observed number of children
Pandits							
Srinagar	72.43	—8.52	—6.22	27.57	11.31	3.12	—3.10
Sopore	27.05	8.36	0.097	72.95	4.35	3.17	3.27
Delhi	80.81	8.88	7.18	19.19	44.74	8.59	15.76
Muslims							
Srinagar	47.16	3.78	1.78	52.84	37.24	19.67	21.46
Sopore	12.84	2.68	0.34	87.16	14.60	12.73	13.07

under consideration for the category of b.c.d. non-users, but among the b.c.d. users this difference is much reduced. Though no population shows a zero difference, a near zero difference is seen among the Muslims of Sopore and Srinagar and the Pandits of Sopore. The two urban Pandit populations (from Srinagar and Delhi respectively), however, show quite contrasting impact. While among the Kashmiri Pandits of Delhi this difference needs to be further reduced by about 9% to become zero, it needs to be increased by about 9% to become zero, among the Kashmiri Pandits of Srinagar. This clearly indicates that the maximum desired impact of the birth control devices is realised among the Kashmiri Pandits of Srinagar and the least among the Kashmiri Pandits of Delhi among the BCD users alone.

Considering the b.c.d. users and non-user together, the weighted differences between the average number of desired and observed number of children have also been calculated in order to understand the totality of the impact of the Family Planning Programmes on the different populations under consideration.

On the population as a whole, the impact of family planning programmes is distinctly seen among the Pandits of Srinagar alone. Among them the average number of children is about 3% lower than the average number of desired children. Following them are the Kashmiri Pandits of Sopore who show about 3% higher average number of the childern than the average of desired children. The remaining three populations show more than 10% increment of the average number of observed children over the average number of desired children. But it is never more than 24% (approximately shown by the Kashmiri Muslims of Sopore).

Sex of the Child preferred and Birth Control

The two important components of the average number of desired children are (1) desired average number of sons (2) desired average number of daughters.

In all the 5 populations under study, the desired average number of sons is much higher than the desired number of daughters in both the categories of parents (users and non-users).

While among the b.c.d. non-users desire for greater number of sons than for daughters seems to have been fulfilled in all the five populations, among the b.c.d. users, this desire is fulfilled only among the Kashmiri Pandits of Srinagar in whom the average number of sons is 1.28 and the average number of daughters is 1.19. In all other population samples the b.c.d. user couples have a higher number of average number of daughters than that of sons.

This (observed ratio of sons and daughters) may be one of the factors responsible for a lower than the desired mean number of children observed among the b.c.d. users of the Kashmiri Pandits of Srinagar, and for non-achievement of the desired impact of birth control practice among the b.c.d. users of the remaining four populations. The fulfilment of the desired ratio of the sex of the children among the b.c.d. non-users may directly be a function of larger average number of children realised than among the b.c.d. users in whom the fertility is deliberately inhibited.

Age-wise Attitude of Women Towards Contraception

Table (3.3) shows that taking the population as a whole 52.15% of these Kashmiri (Pandits & Muslims) samples are averse to using any contraceptive while 47.85% do use these means to limit their family. The overall picture is not very encouraging and much is needed to be done to bring more and more families into the fold of family planning programme.

With respect to the prevalence of users of Birth Control Devices the urban and the non-urban population samples show universally observed variations, the urban Kashmiri Pandits both from Delhi & Srinagar show more than 70% prevalence of birth control devices while the semi-urban Kashmiri Pandits of Sopore show less than 30%.

For the Kashmiri Muslims the prevalence of the use of birth control devices is about 47% for the urban Muslims of Srinagar and about 13% semi-urban Muslims of Sopore.

Thus among the 5 populations, the highest prevalence of birth control devices is seen among the Kashmiri Pandits of Delhi (about 81%) followed by the Kashmiri Pandits of Srinagar (about

Muslims							
Srinagar	15-29	40(40.82)	—	—	9(25.08)	14(35.00)	63
	30-44	38(38.8)	1(100)	3(27.27)	23(65.70)	25(62.50)	90
	45+	20(20.41)	—	8(72.7)	3(8.60)	1(2.50)	32
	Total	98(52.97)	1(0.54)	11(5.94)	35(18.91)	40(21.62)	185
Sopore	15-29	48(37.21)	—	—	1(25)	—	49
	30-44	41(31.78)	1(100)	1(20)	1(25)	9(100)	53
	45+	40(31.01)	—	4(80)	2(50)	—	46
	Total	129(87.18)	1(0.68)	5(3.38)	4(2.70)	9(6.08)	148
	Grand Total	352(52.15)		323	47.85%		

Note : (1) figures in brackets show percentages.
(2) b.c.d. = birth control device.

Further, it is interesting to note that in each of the five Pandit and Muslim populations under study, the percentage of tubectomy exceeds that of vasectomy. In the Pandits of Sopore, it exceeds by 5.74%, in Muslims of Srinagar by 4.96%, in Pandits of Srinagar by 4.32%, in Muslims of Sopore by 2.7% and in Pandits of Delhi by 2.02%. Thus contrary to the existing belief, it is the men who need to be motivated to get sterilised than the women in all these five populations under study.

Condom seems to be the most popular form of contraception prevalent among the Kashmiri Pandits, the percentage of condom users in Delhi, Srinagar and Sopore being 34.35, 34.05 and 11.47 respectively. Users of other methods being 14.14, 13.51, and 9.83 among the Pandits of Delhi, Srinagar and Sopore respectively.

In the case of Muslims the reverse seems to be true, while the condom users are only 19% and 2.7% among the Muslims of Srinagar and Sopore respectively, the users of other methods are 21.49% and 6.08% respectively.

Thus, it may be said that among the Kashmiri Muslims more reliable methods like sterilization and condoms are favoured less than among the Kashmiri Pandits.

Another significant point to be observed is that as high as 87% of Kashmiri Muslim couples and 73% of Kashmiri Pandit couples of Sopore are non-users of birth control devices whatsoever and pose a much greater threat of population explosion compared to their urban counterparts—in whom the frequency of non-users, being about 53% among the Muslims and 19 to 28% among the Pandits. Among the Urban samples it is the Muslims who pose more than 90% risk of population explosion on this score than the Kashmiri Pandits.

In any case the risk of population explosion on account of non-use of birth control devices is greater for the Muslim populations, than for the respective Pandit populations. It is found to be as high as at least 90% for the urban Muslims and about 19% for the semi-urban muslims. For a successful family planning drive among these populations, these relative frequencies of users and non-users of birth control devices have to be born in mind.

Economic Status and Birth Control

Economic status of the families also plays an important role in the attitude towards birth control. Although with the massive family planning programme launched by the Government, the means are available to most of the people free of cost, yet this factor may have effect on the attitudes of people. Economic backwardness goes with educational backwardness and therefore poor are more prone to superstitions, beliefs and misconceived fears against adopting family planning devices. On the other hand there are economically poor people who take to birth control means readily for they know large number of children will spell disaster for their meagre resources.

With a view to studying the impact of economic status on the use of birth control devices, the selected samples have been divided into three economic categories on the basis of median annual per capita income (Please refer to Chapter 2).

Results of income-wise attitude of women towards using birth control devices have been set in Table (3.4).

It is observed that in category 1 (below median) there is a higher percentage of users than non-users among the Pandits of Srinagar and Delhi and among the Muslims of Srinagar.

Among the Pandits and Muslims of Sopore, the frequency of non-users is higher than those of users.

In the category 2 (median) the frequency of users is higher than that of non-users among the Pandits of Srinagar and Delhi.

However, among the Pandits of Sopore and among the Muslims of Srinagar and Sopore there is a higher percentage of non-users than users.

In the category 3 (above median) there is a higher percentage of users than non-users among the Pandits of Srinagar and Delhi, while there is a higher percentage of non-users than users among the Pandits of Sopore and among the Muslims of Srinagar and Sopore.

It is thus apparent that among the urban Pandits the women belonging to all income categories generally use birth control means, while the semi-urban Pandit women belonging to all income categories are least bothered about it.

Table 3.4

Distribution of use of birth control devices by the Kashmiri Pandit and the Muslim spouses respectively according to the Income Category

Population	Income category	Non-users No.	Non-users %	Users No.	Users %
Pandits					
Srinagar	Below Median	19	27.54	50	72.46
	Median	9	28.12	23	71.88
	Above Median	23	27.38	61	72.62
Sopore	Below Median	40	75.47	13	24.53
	Median	15	71.43	6	28.57
	Above Median	34	70.83	14	29.17
Delhi	Below Median	7	17.5	33	82.5
	Median	4	25.0	12	75.0
	Above Median	8	18.60	35	81.4
Muslims					
Srinagar	Below Median	28	43.75	36	56.25
	Median	12	52.17	11	47.83
	Above Median	58	59.18	40	40.82
Sopore	Below Median	40	86.96	6	13.04
	Median	32	86.49	5	13.51
	Above Median	57	87.69	8	12.31

Among the urban Muslims, it is the women of middle and upper income categories only who refrain from the use of any birth control devices. However, among the semi-urban Muslims, it is the women of all income groups who are less bothered about the use of birth control devices.

Therefore, it may be inferreed that no particular trend is observed between the various income levels and the use of birth control devices in the population samples of Kashmiri Pandits and Muslims of Srinagar, Sopore and Delhi.

Thus the finds of the present study corroborate the findings of Majumdar (1960) according to whom, the number of women wishing to restrict the family size does not increase with the income.

Family Type and Birth Control

Traditionally, Kashmiri Pandits have lived in joint families. Comparatively Muslims were found both in nuclear and joint families. Of late, however, the joint family tradition is fast breaking among Pandits also. It has number of reasons. Firstly, for vocational purposes people get disintegrated and even those who would normally live in a joint family have to make their separate hearths and homes. Secondly, tempermentally it has become difficult for people to adjust in a joint family. Among Muslims people having family art or craft or trade tend to live in joint families. Also, Muslims prefer marriages with near relatives. This makes it possible to live together but sometimes leads to quarrels and separation of family members. Economic imbalance among brothers also leads to nuclear living.

In joint family women have to remain under the influence of elders in so far as the use of birth control devices is concerned especially those that cannot be concealed like vasectomy, tubectomy or M. T. P. However, use of pill, condom, jelly, etc. can be made secretly. In a nuclear family, the couple has more freedom to use any birth control device they like.

An attempt has, therefore, been made to find out the effect of the type of family on the use of birth control devices.

Family type-wise, the whole sample of each population under study was divided into two (1) Nuclear Family and (2) Joint Family (Please refer to Chapter 2).

From the Table (3.5), it is observed that in all the urban population samples of Kashmiri Pandits and Muslims, there is a higher percentage frequency of users than non-users among the women of nuclear and joint families. The percentage being higher among nuclear families than among the women belonging to joint families.

As regards semi-urban population samples the percentage of users in both nuclear and joint families is lower than that of non-users. However, even, then the percentage of users is higher in nuclear families than in joint families.

Table 3.5

Distribution of use of birth control devices by the Kashmiri Pandit and the Muslim spouses respectively according to their Family Type

Population	*Family type*	*Non-users*		*Users*	
		No.	*%*	*No.*	*%*
Pandits					
Srinagar	Nuclear	19	24.36	59	75.64
	Joint	32	29.90	75	70.10
Sopore	Nuclear	41	61.19	26	38.81
	Joint	48	87.27	7	12.73
Delhi	Nuclear	6	8.96	61	91.04
	Joint	13	40.62	19	59.38
Muslims					
Srinagar	Nuclear	27	27.55	71	72.45
	Joint	71	81.61	16	18.39
Sopore	Nuclear	36	67.92	17	32.08
	Joint	93	97.89	2	2.11

It is rather apparent that frequency of users of birth control devices is greater in women belonging to nuclear families than in joint families among the urban and semi-urban Kashmiri Pandits and Muslims.

It is to be expected that the higher percentage of BCD users may lead to lower fertility. So, higher the percentage of nuclear families in a population, lower is the fertility.

In view of these findings, maximum increase in the population size may be experienced by the Muslims of Sopore and least by the Pandits of Delhi and Srinagar and rest of the other populations under consideration occupy the intermediary positions.

Education and Birth Control

One of the most important factors that affects the attitude of women towards use of contraception is their level of education. Education not only enables women to acquire knowledge about the various devices of contraception, and their relative merits but also creates awareness for limiting their families and spacing the child-birth. According to Dandekar's (1959) study the education of husbands does not have any effect on the attitude of their wives towards contraception. The education of the woman themselves does affect their attitudes. The ease and freedom with which an educated woman can discuss the family planning methods at least with her husband, an uneducated woman cannot and does not. In this regard our samples are best suited for a study of the effect of education on the attitude towards birth control because whereas the Muslim women have higher percentage with no formal education, Pandits have lesser percentage of women in this group.

From Table 3.6 we observe that with the increase in the level of education of women there is a definite increase in the percentage of those using contraceptives. In all the five populations samples we find that women with no formal education have higher percentage of non-users than users. (Pandits—Srinagar 52.78%, Pandits—Delhi 70.83% and Muslims—Srinagar 75%). At the semi-urban Sopore both Pandit and Muslim women with no formal education are 100% non-users. In the case of Pandits at Srinagar there is a gradual increase in the percentage of users with the increase in level of education from 47.22% for no formal education to 53.55% for Middle education, 75% for secondary level education and 95.45% for Graduate level. There is, however a decrease thereafter to 88.24% for Post-graduate level which may be because of a small number of women in this group. All the women with post-graduate level education at the remaining urban places and semi-urban place use contraceptives. All the graduate Muslim women too both at Sopore and Srinagar use birth control devices. At Delhi Kashmiri Pandit women with

Table 3.6
Distribution of use of birth control devices by the Kashmiri Pandit and the Muslim women respectively according to their education level

Population	Level of Education	Non-users No.	Non-users %	Users No.	Users %
Pandits					
Srinagar	1. No formal education	19	52.78	17	47.22
	2. Middle School	14	46.67	16	53.33
	3. Secondary	14	25.0	42	75.00
	4. Graduate	2	4.55	44	95.45
	5. Post-graduate and above	2	11.76	15	88.24
Sopore	1. No formal education	52	100.0	—	—
	2. Middle School	13	92.86	1	7.14
	3. Secondary	12	38.71	19	61.29
	4. Graduate	9	47.37	10	52.63
	5. Post-graduate and above	—	—	3	100.0
Delhi	1. No formal education	17	70.83	7	29.17
	2. Middle School	2	13.33	13	86.67
	3. Secondary	—	—	26	100.0
	4. Graduate	—	—	22	100.00
	5. Post-graduate and above	—	—	12	100.00
Muslims					
Srinagar	1. No formal education	93	75.0	31	25.0
	2. Middle School	3	11.11	24	88.89
	3. Secondary	2	12.5	14	87.5
	4. Graduate	—	—	3	100.00
	5. Post-graduate and above	—		15	100.0
Sopore	1. No formal education	110	100	11	78.57
	2. Middle School	7	100	—	—
	3. Secondary	3	21.43	11	78.57
	4 Graduate	—		6	100
	5. Post-graduate and above	—		2	100

education of Secondary level and above are found to use contraceptives of one sort or the other.

Thus it can be concluded that with the increase in the level of education of women we can bring into the fold of family planning and birth control programme, large number of women and reduce the birth rate to the desired levels, though much higher level of education would be needed for Muslim women than for the Kashmiri Pandit women.

CHAPTER

4

Urban and Semi-Urban Population Variation in Fertility and Mortality

FERTILITY

BIRTH IS the result of mating between males and females. The frequency of these births forms the basis for measuring fertility. To measure fertility various methods may be adopted, some of which though sophisticated are complex but each is related to others to a greater or a lesser degree. The following methods for estimating fertility as stated by Barclay (1958) were used :

I. Child-woman Ratio

This is a ratio of children in the age interval of 0-4 years to every 1000 women of child-bearing age (15-49 years). This method cannot be considered very accurate as the number of births which are noted are survivors rather than the actual number of births. Yet this measure of fertility is useful particularly when the population births are not registered regularly. The formula used is $\frac{P_{0-4}}{F_{15-49}} X\ K$, where P_{0-4} is the number of children of both sexes, in the age-interval of 0-4 years. F_{15-49} is the number of females of child-bearing age of 15-49 years and K is 1000.

It is observed that the semi-urban Pandit population has a higher child woman ratio than the urban Pandit samples. The differences being significant between semi-urban Pandits and urban

Pandits of Srinagar and Delhi respectively ($X^2=8.9171$, d.f.$=1$; $.017>P>.001$; $X^2=6.8695$, d.f.$=1$, $.01>P>.001$ respectively).

Table 4.1 shows the child-woman ratio of various populations under study.

Table 4.1

Child-Woman Ratio among the urban and the semi-urban Kashmiri Pandits and Muslims

Population	*No. of children (0-4 years)*	*No. of women (15-49 years)*	*Child-woman Ratio*
Pandits			
Srinagar	43	161	267.1
Sopore	55	101	544.5
Delhi	18	73	246.5
Muslims			
Srinagar	81	170	476.5
Sopore	81	126	642.5

The urban Muslim population also has a lower child woman ratio than the semi-urban Muslim population, the difference being statistically not significant ($X^2=0.6369$, d. f. $= 1$, $.50 > P > .30$). Further, no significant differences in child woman ratio were obtained between the urban Pandits of Srinagar and the migrant Pandits of Delhi ($X^2 = 0.0651$, d. f. $= 1$, $.80 > P > .70$).

In comparison to the national average of 65.9, based on 1961 census (Jones, 1974) it is seen that the child-woman ratio is lower, both in urban and semi-urban population samples of the two communities under study.

II. Crude Birth Rate

This rate is worked out by dividing the number of births during the year by the average or mid-year population (calculated on the basis of nuclear family sizes) and multiplying by 1000. Table 4.2 gives a comparative picture of the urban and the semi-urban populations of Kashmiri Pandits and Muslims.

Table 4.2

Crude-Birth Rate of the urban and the semi-urban Kashmiri Pandits and Muslims

Population	*No. of live births*	*Total popu-lation*	*Crude Birth Rate*
Pandits			
Srinagar	9	638	14.11
Sopore	14	606	23.10
Delhi	7	292	23.97
Muslims			
Srinagar	21	1020	20.58
Sopore	30	882	34.01

It is observed that the semi-urban samples of both the communities have higher crude birth rate than that of their urban counterparts. In case of urban Pandits, it is the Delhi Pandits which have the higher crude birth rate. But these variations were not found to be statistically significant (*a*) $X^2=3.466$; d.f.$=1$, $.10>P>.05$; (*b*) $X^2=0.664$, d.f.$=1$, $.50>P>.30$; (*c*) $X^2=0.654$, d.f.$=1$, $.50>P>.30$; (*d*) $X^2=0.650$, d.f.$=1$, $.50>P>.30$).

III. General Fertility Rate

In addition to the Crude Birth Rate, General Fertility Rate has also been calculated. The essential difference between the two is that Crude Birth Rate is the ratio of a year's registered births to the total mid-year population, but the General Fertility Rate is the ratio of total yearly registered births to the population of women of child-bearing age i.e. the age-group of 15-49 years. The formula adopted is B/P_1K, where B is the number of live births registered during the year, P_1 is the mid-year population of women between 15-49 years and K is 1000.

From Table 4.3, it is seen that in case of General Fertility Rate, too, the semi-urban Pandits and Muslims have higher rates than that of their urban counterparts. But these

Table 4.3

General Fertility Rate of the urban and the semi-urban Kashmiri Pandits and Muslims

Population	*No. of live births*	*No. of women (15-49) years*	*General Fertility Rate*
Pandits			
Srinagar	9	161	55.9
Sopore	14	101	138.61
Delhi	7	73	95.9
Muslims			
Srinagar	21	170	123.53
Sopore	30	126	238.1

differences were found to be significant only between urban Pandit population of Srinagar and semi-urban Pandits of Sopore (X^2=4.2778, d.f.=1, .05>P>.02); no significant differences were found between urban Pandit population of Delhi and semi-urban Pandits of Sopore (X^2=0.5877, d.f.=1, .50>P>.30) and between urban and semi-urban Muslims (X^2=0.3826, d.f.=1, .70>P>.50). Further, though it was found that the migrant urban Pandits of Delhi have higher General Fertility Rate than that of urban Pandits of Srinagar, this difference was found to be not significant (X =1.0336, d.f.=1, .50>P>.30).

IV. Age-Specific Fertility Rates

In recent years anthropologists have started evincing interest in male fertility rates as well (Damon and Thomas, 1967), yet, age-specific fertility rates are still meant to refer to women only. This rate is arrived at by dividing the number of live births of mothers by the number of women of that age and multiplying by 1000. Typically demographers group the data into 5 years age-groups rather than using single year rates. The formula used is $b_1/p_1 k$, where b_1 refers to the number of births registered during the year to women in the age-interval, p_1 is the mid-year population of women in the same age-interval and K is 1000.

Table 4.4

Age-Specific Birth Rates of the urban and the semi-urban Kashmiri Pandits and Muslims

Population	*Age groups* 15-19	20-24	25-29	30-34	35-39	40-44	45-49
Pandits							
Srinagar	0	400.00	90.90	0	0	0	0
Sopore	0	375.00	259.25	148.14	0	0	0
Delhi	0	333.33	500.00	333.33	0	0	0
Muslims							
Srinagar	333.33	500.00	97.56	56.6	90.91	0	71.43
Sopore	333.33	588.23	413.79	304.34	0	0	0

This method is considered to be more accurate as emphasis is laid on specific time period of live births to women.

Table 4.4 and figure (4) reveals the age specific birth rates of the urban and semi-urban populations, respectively for Pandits and Muslims. It is a fact accepted by the demographers that the rate of child-bearing is not uniform throughout the reproductive years. The age-specific birth rates obtained through the National Sample Survey (1963) as well as the All India 1971 census, show that the fertility of the Indian women reaches its peak in the age-group 20-24 which means that the Indian fertility is of "early peak-type" (Census of India, 1971). According to 1961 census estimation done by Agarwal (1973) the maximum risk of producing children is from the mothers in the age of 20-34 years. The study conducted on Delhi population in 1969-70 also shows that the peak child bearing is in the age-interval of 20-24 years whereafter it declines steadily up to 35-39 years age-group.

The present study reveals that the peak child-bearing period among the urban (except the migrant urban Pandits) as well as the semi-urban Pandits and Muslims conforms to the figures obtained through National Sample Survey (1963) and the All India Census (1971). The migrant population of Pandits at Delhi, however, shows the peak in the age-group of 25-29 years instead of 20-24 years.

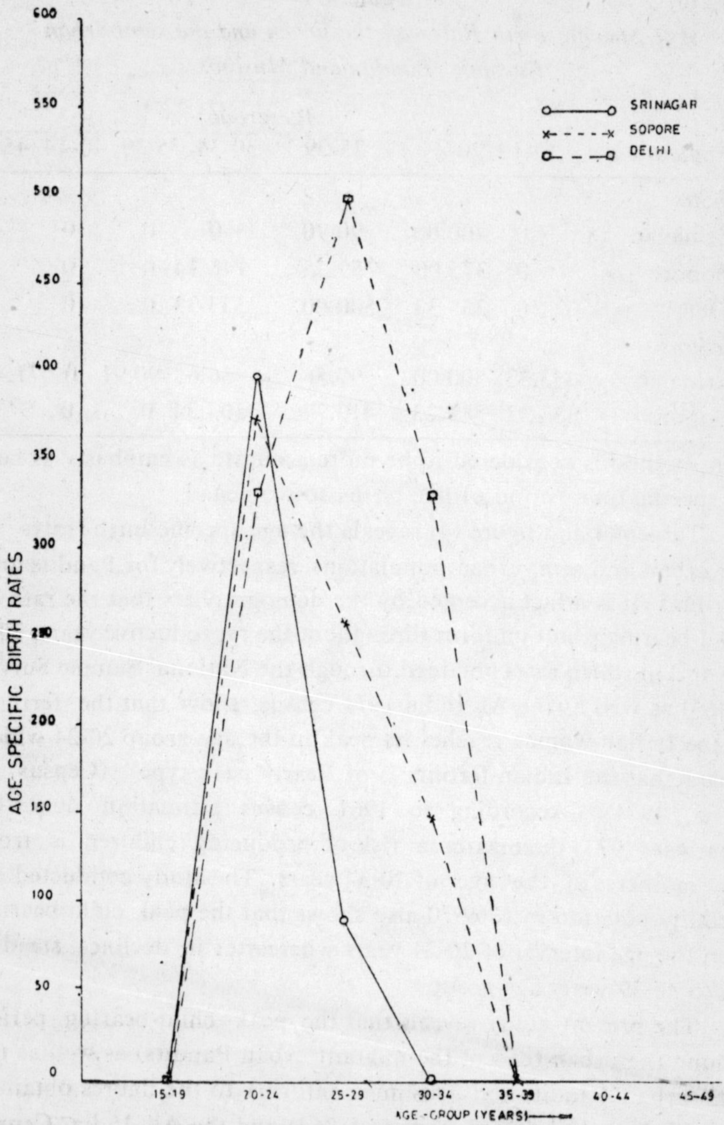

Fig. 4(a). Specific Birth Rates among the urban and semi-urban Kashmiri Pandits

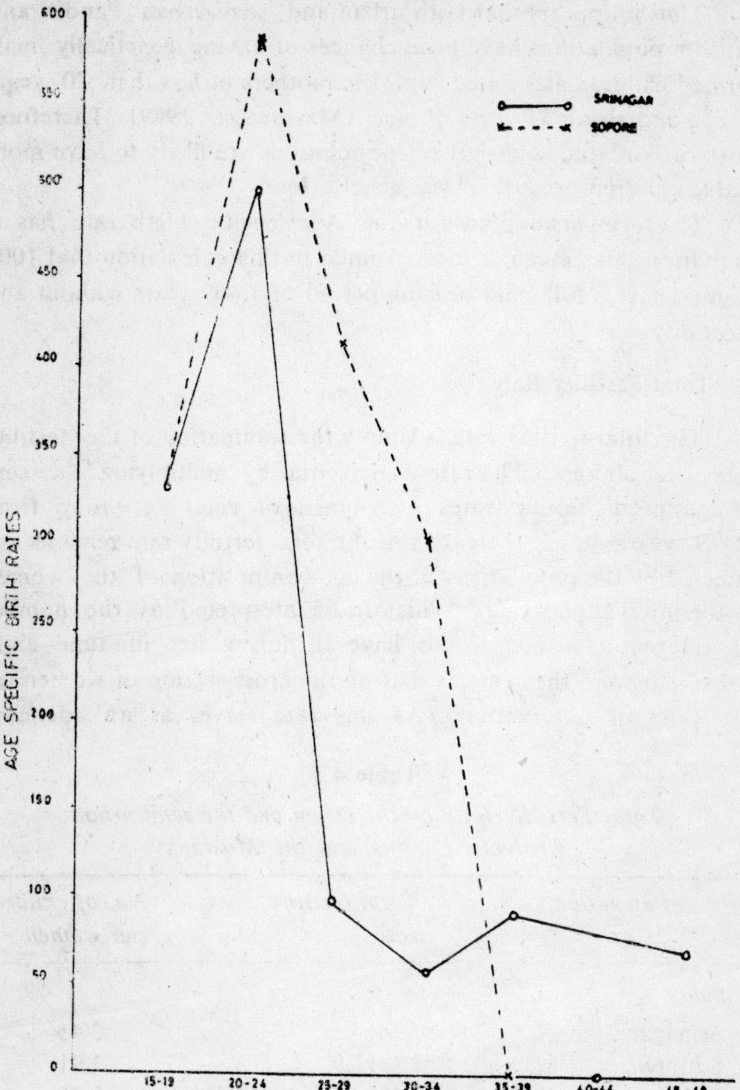

Fig. 4(b). Age specific birth rates among the urban and semi-urban Kashmiri Muslims

Thus it appears that both urban and semi-urban Pandit and Muslim populations have little chances of having genetically malformed children associated with the mothers of less than 20 years of age and above 34 years of age (Matsunaga, 1969). Therefore, both urban and semi-urban populations are likely to have more viable children because of less genetic load.

The formula adopted for the Age-specific birth rate has a limitation in as much as it is assumed in this calculation that 1000 women have a full child bearing period of 15-49 years without any mortality.

V. Total Fertility Rate

The total fertility rate is simply the summation of the fertility rates over all ages. The rate is arrived at by multiplying the sum of age-specific fertility rates of women of each age-group from 15-49 years by 5. Due to this the total fertility rate remains unaffected by the peculiarities of the age-composition of the women in the interval of 5 years. This can be interpreted as the number of children a woman would have if during her life-time child behaviour were the same as that of the cross-section of women at the time of observation. As this rate serves as an adequate

Table 4.5

Total Fertility Rate of the urban and the semi-urban Kashmiri Pandits and the Muslims

Population	*Total fertility rate*	*No. of children per women*
Pandits		
Srinagar	2454.5	2.45
Sopore	3911.9	3.91
Delhi	5833.3	5.83
Muslims		
Srinagar	5749.15	5.75
Sopore	8198.5	8.20

approximation of actual average completed family size, it is an accepted measure of level of fertility.

TFR = 5 *X* sum of five-years age-group fertility rates. Table 4.5 shows the intra group comparison of Total fertility rates as also that of the number of children per women.

It is observed that the semi-urban pandits and muslims have higher total fertility rates than that of their urban counterparts in Srinagar.

It is observed that the average number of children per women in case of Pandits is highest among the urban Pandits of Delhi (5.83), followed by that of semi-urban Pandits (3.91) and least in the urban Pandits of Srinagar (2.45).

However, in case of Muslims, the semi-urbans have much higher average number of children per woman (8.2) than among the urbans (5.75).

In view of these figures, it seems that the parents among the urban Pandits of Srinagar are almost replacing themselves while among the semi-urban Pandits, they are nearly doubling themselves and in the migrant urban pandits of Delhi, they are more than doubling themselves.

In case of Muslims, the urban parents are replacing themselves by nearly three times while the semi-urban parents are doing so by four times.

Thus only the urban Pandit population of Srinagar is eventually likely to become almost stable sooner. Rest of the other urban and semi-urban Pandit and Muslim populations seem to be ever growing in size.

Further, it may be inferred that urban, semi-urban factor does not seem to be responsible for the variations observed with respect to total fertility rate among the Pandits, while, this may be an important factor influencing total fertility among the Muslims of Kashmir.

VI. Cumulative Natality Rate

Cumulative Natality Rates estimate the number of children that 1000 women of an age-group would deliver from the time

Table 4.6

Cumulative Natality Rate among the urban and the semi-urban Kashmiri Pandits and Muslims

Population	*Age groups (years)*						
	15-19	20-24	25-29	30-34	35-39	40-44	45-49
Pandits							
Srinagar	0	2000	2459.50	2454.50	2454.50	2454.50	2454.50
Sopore	0	1875	3171.25	3911.95	3911 95	3911.95	3911.95
Delhi	0	1666.65	4166.65	5833.3	5833.3	5833.3	5833.3
Muslims							
Srinagar	1666.65	4166.65	4654.45	4937.45	5392.0	5392.0	5749.15
Sopore	1666.65	4607.00	6676.75	8198.45	8198.45	8198.45	8198 45

they began child bearing until they reach a specified age, if they were exposed to the age-specific birth rates in effect at a given time.

The cumulative Natality rate is calculated by multiplying the age-specific birth rate of each 5 year age-group by 5 and adding the product of the age-specific birth rate of the next 5 years age-group.

From the table 4.6 it is seen that the cumulative Natality Rate of Pandits at Srinagar becomes stable from the age-group 25-29 years onwards while that of sem-urban Pandits and of migrant Pandits of Delhi, it attains stability from the age-group 30-34 years onwards. Among the Muslims the semi-urbans show stability from 30-34 years age-group while the urbans show no stability.

VII. Gross Reproduction Rate

Total fertility rate includes all births, both male and female and consequently does not give an estimate of the potential breeders (women) in a population in future. Therefore, another measure of fertility-the Gross Reproduction Rate is calculated which shows how many girl babies—potential future mothers would be born to 1000 women passing through their child-bearing years, if the age-specific birth rate of a given year remained constant and if no woman entering the child-bearing period died before reaching the menopausal age. This rate is calculated by multiplying total fertility by the ratio of the females to the total births. If the product is 1000 or more it means that more daughters are being born by each of 1000 women of child-bearing age without taking into consideration the deaths of women during their reproductive period.

From the table 4.7, it is observed that among both the urban as well as the semi-urban Pandits the Gross reproduction rate being less than 1000, less daughters are born. But among the muslims, the urban as well as the semi-urbans, Gross reproduction rate being above 1000, more daughters are being born by each of 1000, women of child-bearing age. In fact, the semi-urban muslims have higher gross reproduction rate than that of the urban muslims

Table 4.7

Gross Reproduction Rate among the urban and the semi-urban Kashmiri Pandits and Muslims

Population	*Gross Reproduction Rate*
Pandits	
Srinagar	818.16
Sopore	838.28
Delhi	833.33
Muslims	
Srinagar	1642.61
Sopore	4099.22

In the case of former, 4 girls are born to every woman of child-bearing age while 2 girls are born to every woman of child-bearing age in the latter-the variation found is not significant ($X^2=1.03$, d.f.$=1$, $.50>p>.30$). In case of Pandits also, the variations found between urbans and semi-urbans are not significant.

Therefore, it may be inferred that in view of such rates of Gross reproduction among urban and semi-urban Pandits and Muslims, the urban and semi-urban Pandit populations are under the threat. of severe deficiency of females in the reproductive age group leading to the shrinking of this population.

However, the urban and especially semi-urban populations seem to have a surplus of future mothers, imposing a great threat of population explosion.

Genetically, there is likely to be a reduction in the frequency of X-linked recessive lethal genes in the urban and semi-urban Pandit populations while in the urban and especially semi-urban muslim populations there is likely to be an increase in the frequency of such genes which is, however, likely to be countered by the effects of consanguinity and inbreeding which is quite prevalent among the muslims and is almost non-existent among the Pandits.

Age at Menarche and at Menopause

With the onset of menstruation women assume fertility. This stage known as menarche, marks a definite uterine development and signifies sexual maturity. Cessation of menstrual flow is known as menopause. It is this span between menstrual and menopause that is known as the reproductive period in a woman's life and pregnancy can occur at any time during this period (Mamoria, 1965)

Various investigations reveal that the factors like nutrition and heredity etc. contribute towards the observed variation in age at menarche in different populations. Tanner (1960) reports a very large degree of biological variability and most of it is due to genetic causes. He mentions that the menarcheal age depends on the combined action of genes at many different loci rather than any single gene.

The variation in the menarcheal age has considerable effect on the reproductive life of a woman and therefore deserves some consideration.

Table (4.8a) reveals the percentage frequency of all women by age at which they had experienced menarche in the urban and semi urban Pandit and Muslim populations.

It is observed that the highest frequency of women among the urban and the semi-urban Pandits and Muslims is found in the age group of 14 years, followed by those in age-group 15 years (Pandits) and 13 years (Muslims).

Further, it is seen from table (4.8 b) that the mean age at menarche is around 14 years of age in all the urban and semi-urban Pandit and Muslim populations.

Thus it may be inferred that on account of age at menarche, the urban Pandits and Muslims do not differ much from their semi-urban counterparts.

Table 4.8 (a)

Percentage frequency of women by the age at menarche in urban and semi-urban Kashmiri Pandits and Muslims

Population	*Age at Menarche (years)*								
	11	*12*	*13*	*14*	*15*	*16*	*17*	*18*	*19*
Pandits									
Srinagar	3.24	10.8	15.7	30.0	33.3	5.4	0.54	0.54	0 54
Sopore	0.82	7.4	13.9	40.2	22.1	11.5	2.5	0.0	1.64
Delhi	2.02	7.07	17.17	36.4	26.3	7.1	2.02	1.01	1.01
Muslims									
Srinagar	2.16	10.27	27.57	34.59	15.67	8.65	0.54	0.54	0.0
Sopore	2.03	12.16	23.65	37.84	18.24	3.38	1.35	0.67	0.67

Table 4.8 (b)

Mean Age at Menarche among the urban and semi-urban Kashmiri Pandits and Muslims

Population	*Age at Menarche*		
	Mean	*S.D.*	*S.E.*
Pandits			
Srinagar	14.01	1.29	0.09
Sopore	14.29	1.32	0.12
Delhi	14.18	1.32	0.13
Muslims			
Srinagar	13.82	1.22	0.09
Sopore	13.81	1.20	0.10

Table 4.9(a)

Percentage distribution of women by the age at menopause in urban and semi-urban Kashmiri Pandits and Muslims

Populatation	*Age at Menopause (years)*								
	<40	41-42	43-44	45-46	47-48	49-50	51-52	53-54	55+
Pandits									
Srinagar	6.45	6.45	3.23	22.58	19.35	29.03	6.45	3.23	3.23
Sopore	4.17	8.33	4.17	16.67	20.83	4.17	4.17	4.17	8.32
Delhi	0.0	0.0	2.86	8.57	22.86	14.29	25.71	14.29	11.42
Muslims									
Srinagar	3.85	3.85	7.69	11.54	19.23	23.08	15.37	11.54	3.85
Sopore	0.0	6.90	3.45	6.9	6.9	24.14	34.48	6.9	10.33

Table 4.9(b)

Mean age at Menopause among the urban and the semi-urban Kashmiri Pandits and Muslims

Population	Age at menopause in year		
	Mean	S D.	S E
Pandits			
Srinagar	47.31	3.64	0.65
Sopore	47.83	3.95	0.81
Delhi	50.3	3.12	0.53
Muslims			
Srinagar	48.5	3.81	0.75
Sopore	49.9	3.62	0.67

Table (4.9a) reveals that among the Pandits, the semi-urban Pandits of Sopore and the urban Pandits of Srinagar have maximum percentage frequency of women in the age group 49-50 years while the migrant urban Pandits of Delhi have the highest percentage of women in the age group 51-52 years.

In case of Muslims, the urban have the maximum percentage frequency of women in the age group 49-50 years, while the semi-urbans have in the next age group—the 51-52 years.

With respect to mean age at menopause (table 4.9b) the urban Pandits of Delhi have the highest mean age at menopause (50.3 years) followed by the semi-uraban Pandits (47.83 years) and least in the urban Pandits of Srinagar.

The semi-urban Muslims have the higher mean age at menopause (49.9 years) than the urbans (48.5).

Thus, it may be said that the urban, semi-urban differences do not hold true in case of Pandits with respect of age at menopause.

But in Muslims, the urban and semi-urban population samples do show variation with respect to age at menopause.

Reproductive span

From the results thus obtained, about the mean age at menarche and mean age at menopause, the reproductive span

Table 4.10

Conceptions and Conception wastage among the semi-urban Kashmiri Pandits and Muslims

Population	Total No. of women	Total concep-tions	Average No. of concep-tions	Number of						
				Living children	Dead before 20 yrs. of age	Abortions		Mis-carriage	Still births	Preg-nancy
						Induced	Spon-taneous			
Pandits										
Srinagar	185	587	3.17	486 (82.79)	25 (4.26)	5 (0.85)	58 (9.88)	6 (1.02)	1 (0.17)	6 (1.02)
Sopore	122	444	3.64	370 (83.33)	27 (6.08)	2 (0.45)	23 (5.18)	11 (2.48)	2 (0.45)	9 (2.02)
Delhi	99	365	3.69	299 (81.92)	15 (4.10)	26 (7.12)	18 (4.93)	4 (1.09)	0	3
Muslims										
Srinagar	185	786	4.25	653 (83.08)	61 (7.76)	0	50 (6.36)	18 (2.29)	2 (0.25)	2 (0.25)
Sopore	148	629	4.25	503 (79.97)	59 (9.38)	0	45 (7.15)	14 (2.23)	5 (0.79)	3 (0.48)

Note : Figures in brackets show percentages.

among Pandits seems to be longest among the women of the urban Pandit of Delhi (36.1 years), followed by the semi-urban Pandits (33.54 years) and shortest in the Pandits of Srinagar (33.3 years).

In case of Muslims, the semi-urban population sample has the longer reproductive period (36.1 years) than the urban sample (34.7 years).

Consequently, it may be inferred that in case of Kashmiri Pandits, the urban and semi-urban factor is not responsible for the variations in the reproductive span.

However, in case of Muslims the urban and semi-urban factor seems to be responsible for the difference in the reproductive span.

Thus it appears, that from the fertility point of view, the semi-urban Muslims and the urban Pandits of Delhi are much more likely to contribute to the future population growth.

Conceptions

The results of conceptions of the Kashmiri Pandit and the Muslim women have been set out in table (4.10). The average number of conceptions is found to be highest among the semi-urban (4.25) and the urban (4.25) Muslims followod by that of migrant urban Pandits (3.69) and the semi-urban Pandits (3.64) and least is found among the urban Pandits from Srinagar (3.17). No significant differences were found between the semi-urban and urban Pandit and Muslim population samples.

Mortality

As has been explained elsewhere, the net result of the increase in population is the interaction of fertility and mortality. It is, therefore, of paramount importance to study the position of pre-natal and post-natal deaths vis-a-vis the number of living children.

The three tables (4.11, 4.12, 4.13) give the distribution of pre-natal deaths, post-natal deaths and live borns among the urban and the semi-urban Pandits and Muslims. For purposes of pre-natal deaths—miscarriages, still births and spontaneous abortions

Table 4.11

Distribution of pre-natal deaths, post-natal deaths and Living children among the urban and semi-urban Kashmiri Pandits and Muslims

Population	*Pre-Natal deaths*		*Post-Natal deaths*		*Living children*	
	No.	*%*	*No.*	*%*	*No.*	*%*
Pandits						
Srinagar	65	11.07	25	4.26	486	81.09
Sopore	36	8.11	27	6.08	370	86.26
X^2	3.93	d.f.=2;	.20>P>.10			
Pandits						
Srinagar	65	11.07	25	4.26	486	81.09
Sopore	22	6.02	415	4.10	299	76.16
X^2	5.80	d.f.=2;	.10>P>.05			
Pandits						
Sopore	36	8.11	27	6.08	370	86.26
Delhi	22	6.02	15	4.10	299	76.16
X^2	2.16	d.f.=2;	.05>P>.30			
Muslims						
Srinagar	70	8.91	61	7.76	653	83.08
Sopore	64	10.27	59	9.38	503	79.97
X^2	1.48	d.f.=2;	.50>P>.30			

have been taken into account and for post-natal deaths – all non-accidental deaths prior to 21 years of age has been considered.

It was observed that none of semi-urban population samples exhibited any significant variation from that of their urban counterparts. Only exception being that of urban Pandits of Delhi who have much lower percentage of pre-natal deaths than the urban Pandits of Srinagar—the difference being significant (X^2 = 5.81, d.f. = 1, .02 > P > .01).

Table 4.12

Distribution of Pre-natal deaths, Live borns among the urban and the semi-urban Kashmiri Pandits and Muslims

Population		Pre-Natal deaths		Live borns	
		No.	*%*	*No.*	*%*
Pandits					
Srinagar		65	11.07	511	87.05
Sopore		36	8.11	397	89.41
X^2	2.45	d.f.=1,	.20>P>.10		
Pandits					
Srinagar		65	11.07	511	87.05
Delhi		22	6.02	314	86.02
X^2	5.81	d.f.=1;	.002>P>.01		
Pandits					
Sopore		36	8.11	397	89.41
Delhi		22	6.02	314	86.02
X^2	0.85	d.f.=1;	.50>P>.30		
Muslims					
Srinagar		70	8.21	714	90.84
Sopore		64	10.27	562	89.35
X^2	0.38	d.f.=1;	.70>P>.50		

Table 4.13

Distribution of Post-Natal Deaths and Live borns among the urban and semi-urban Kashmiri Pandits and Muslims

Population		Non-accidental Post-natal deaths		Live borns	
		No.	%	*No.*	%
Pandits					
Srinagar		25	4.26	511	87.05
Sopore		27	6.08	397	89.41
X^2	1 332	d.f.=1	.30>P>.02		
Pandits					
Srinagar		25	4.26	511	87.05
Delhi		15	4.10	314	86.02
X^2	0.006	d.f.=1;	.98>P>.95		
Pandits					
Sopore		27	6.08	397	89.41
Delhi		15	4.10	314	86.02
X^2	1.171	d.f.=1;	.30>P>.20		
Muslims					
Srinagar		61	7.76	714	90.84
Sopore		59	9 38	562	89.35
X^2	1.16	d.f.=1;	.30>P>.20		

Table 4 14

Fertility and Mortality Indices among the urban and semi-urban Kashmiri Pandits and Muslims

Population	Child birth index	Survival index	Child loss index	Abortion rate/100	Miscarriage rate/100	Still birth rate/100
Pandits						
Srinagar	2.76	2.63	0.14	9.88	1.02	0.17
Sopore	3.25	3.03	0.22	5.18	2.48	0.45
Delhi	3.17	3.02	0.15	4.93	1.10	—
Muslims						
Srinagar	3.86	3.53	0.33	6.36	2.29	0.25
Sopore	3.80	3.40	0.40	7.15	2.33	0.79

Intra population comparisons

It is seen from the table 4.14 that among the Pandits the semi-urban population has the highest child birth index and survival index followed by the urban Pandits of Delhi and by the urban Pandits of Srinagar, while among Muslims the urbans have marginally higher indices than that of semi-urbans. The child-loss index is higher among the semi-urban counterparts. The abortion rate is higher among the urban Pandits of Srinagar but lower among the urban Pandits of Delhi than among that of their semi-urban counterparts, while among Muslims, the reverse is true. From these figures it appears that the pre-natal selection is more intense in case of urban Pandits of Srinagar and post-natal selection is more intense among semi-urban Muslims.

Bio-social Factors

Fertility has been defined as an indicator of the actual reproductive performance of a woman or groups of a women (Lewis and Thompson 1965). Bernard Benjamin (1969) defines it as a measure of the rate at which a population adds to itself by births. It is different from fecundity which is a physiological capacity to participate in reproduction. Even though birth is a biological process yet birth rate is influenced by many factors including social, economic, religious and moral. In the past there was no check or control on child producing but today the fertility is being checked; most of the urban and elite sections of people wish to have limited family. According to Prof. Burten Bendict (1973) "If there is one thing which experience with family planning has shown, it is that people are not motivated to limit their families by population statistics or even by the ease or availabiltiy of contraceptives but by a whole set of social factors impinging on their personal lives and changing over their life cycles."

Besides genetically determined incompatability and morbidity the more important of the biological factors affecting fertility is the health—the related factors being disease, food habits etc. As the health improves, the death rate comes down. With the provision of and utilisation by the people of sufficient health facilities, the death rate has come down considerably. The death rate for the whole of India which was 47.2 during the decade 1911-20 has come down to 15.9 in 1969-70. The death rate in Jammu and Kashmir State during the year 1969-70 was only 13.2. In this context it would be interesting to report the expectation of life at selected ages by sex in Jammu & Kashmir in relation to that in India as a whole.

Table 4.15

Life Expectancy of the Population of Jammu & Kashmir State and of India (as a whole) (1951-61)

Population	*Expectation of life at ages (in years)*						
	0	*1*	*5*	*10*	*20*	*40*	*70*
Male							
J & K	37.65	43.88	44.21	41.06	33.35	20.43	7.05
India	41.39	47.82	48.14	44.08	35.42	21.16	7.14
Female							
J & K	35.81	40.26	39.74	36.73	29.65	18.41	6.99
India	40.00	45.47	45.76	42.11	33.68	20.57	7.41

It is seen that the expectation of life in Jammu & Kashmir has been less than that in the country as a whole both for males and females.

Several attempts have been made to study differential rate of fertility among various sections of population in India. Studies have been made to find out the relationship of fertility with education, income, religion, duration of married life, age of the mothers and other factors. After analysing the census data of 1931 and 1941, Davis (1951) has come to the conclusion that there is marked difference between the fertility in large cities, small townships and rural areas. However, many other studies have concluded that the rural-urban differential is small and insignificant (Raina 1969). Wattal (1958) maintained that in the West there is some relationship between education and fertility but in India, on the basis of small data, it is very difficult to derive any conclusions.

Agarwal (1966) feels that education does affect the fertility but only when the level among women is of Matriculation or more. According to Mitra (1970), however, education plays a decisive role in restricting the family size. In the study carried out by Majumdar (1960) no relationship between income and fertility was found, while relationship between fertility and religion was discernible. Pati and Dutta's work (1958) is significant in as much as relationship has been established between social mobility, family types and reproductive rate. Dandekar (1959) has not been able to find any effect on fertility performance of any of the factors like age at marriage, age difference between the husband and the wife, income, duration of married life or caste. On the other hand, Bhowmik et al (1971) after a study on Zemi women of Nagaland did find some relationship between these factors and fertility performance. In the survey of Mysore (U.N. 1961) it was concluded that rural females marrying between the ages of 14 and 17 produce 5.9 children on an average while those marrying between the ages of 18 and 21 produce only 4.7 children on an average. However, small difference in the ages at marriage does not materially affect fertility (Krishnamoorthy, 1968). Among the foreign scholars who have conducted studies on differential fertility, Thompson (1953) has covered USA, England and Wales, France, Germany and Sweden and Cox (1970) has studied the position in Britain, besides carrying out a study of general fertility in India, China and Japan.

Mother's age, Parity and Frequency of Children

Age of mothers is highly correlated with number of pregnancies, younger women have fewer and older women have more number of children (Stern C, 1968).

It is well known that certain types of chromosomal abnormalities such as Group G trisomy, XXY and XXX occur in association with increased maternal age. The frequency of Mongolian idiocy, harelip with or without cleft plate and many other abnormalities, caused by either mutant genes or chromosomal aberrations abruptly increase after 24 years of maternal age. Some other abnormalities e.g., spine bifide, pyloric stenosis etc., are more common in the children of younger mothers (Roy and Ghosh, 1972).

A variety of congenital defects such as Rherythroblostosis, strasbisums and other malformations of the nervous system and sense organs are manifested increasingly with advancing birth order. There are still other defects like cerebral palsy, congenital malformation of the circulatory system which show the effect of advancing maternal age as well as birth order (Newcombe, 1964). Thus it would be expected that the incidence of a variety of congenital defects may be reduced as a result of decreasing frequencies of births of higher ranks as well as those of younger mothers. According to the analysis carried out by Matsunaga (1969) of the statistics of 1956 of Japan, the rate of still births increases very significantly in mothers below 19 years and above 35 years of age as well as with high order of birth.

There is a connection between the frequency of chondrodystrophic mutations and age of mothers, Older mothers have a significantly higher relative rate of mutant births. It is possible, however, that it is the higher age of father rather than of the mother which is responsible. In that case, too, the mother's age is

Table 4.16

Mean age of mothers at Different parities among the urban and the semi-urban Kashmiri Pandits and Muslims

Population	*Mean age of mothers at the time of birth of children in years at parity*								*Mean interval between parities in yeors.*
	0	*I*	*II*	*III*	*IV*	*V*	*VI*	*VII*	
Pandits									
Srinagar	20.96	23.79	25.72	28.89	32.42	37.40	39.5	44.0	3.29
Sopore	21.02	23.68	26.2	29.04	31.31	33.81	28.6	—	2.93
Delhi	21.4	24.04	25.96	28.53	30.11	31.75	—	—	2.07
Muslims									
Srinagar	21.37	22.17	24.26	26.90	29.20	32.90	33.12	35.20	1.97
Sopore	20.67	22.71	24.89	27.54	29.30	30.58	31.30	35.66	2.14

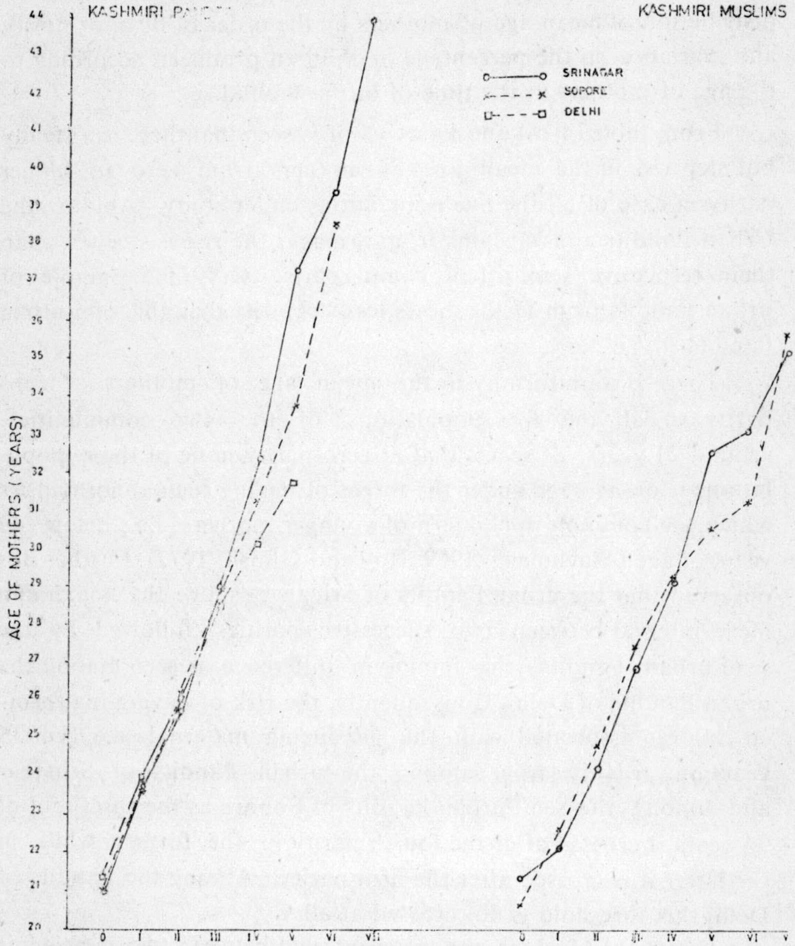

Fig. 5. Mother's age and parity among urban and semi-urban Pandits and Muslim populations

important because older women have generally older husbands (Stern, 1968).

In the present study an attempt has been made to assess the distribution of mean age of mothers by the order of birth or parity and variance in the percentage of children produced according to the age of mothers at the time of birth of child.

From table (4.16) and figure (5) it is seen that there is a steady but step rise in the mean age of mothers from zero to higher parity in case of all the five populations under study. Among the Urban Pandits and Muslims from Srinagar the rise is steeper than their respective semi-urban counterparts. Only the sample of urban Pandits from Delhi shows less steep rise than the semi-urban Pandits.

There is a uniformity in the mean age of mothers at zero parity of all the five populations of the two communities-around 21 years. It seems that at zero parity none of these populations is on average under the threat of having such abnormalities which are common in childern of younger mothers i.e. below 19 years of age (Matsunaga 1969; Roy and Ghosh, 1972). Further it is observed that the urban Pandits of Srinagar show the maximum mean interval between two successive parities, followed by the semi-urban Pandits; the minimum difference is seen among the urban Pandits of Delhi. Consequently, the risk of having malformed children associated with the advancing maternal age (i.e. 35 years onwards) is earlier among the urban Pandits of Srinagar and among the semi-urban Pandits of Sopore as the threshold of 34 years is crossed after the fourth parity in the former while in the latter it is crossed after the fifth parity. Among the Pandits of Delhi this threshold is not crossed at all.

In case of Muslims, the mean interval between two parities is almost two years in both urban as well as in semi-urban populations. As a result the fence of 34 years is crossed after the sixth parity in both the urbans and the semi-urban populations, thus showing similar risk of having children with a variety of congenital defects associated with the children borne to older mother (i.e. above 34 years of age).

From table (4.17) and figure (6) it seems the urban Pandits of Delhi have the highest percentage frequency of children born to women aged 20 to 34 years followed by Pandits of Srinagar and the semi-urban Pandits of Sopore successively. Highest percentage frequency of children born to mothers below the age of 20 years is in the urban Pandits of Srinagar; this is followed by the semi-urban Pandits; this is least among the urban Pandits of Delhi. The percentage frequency of children born to mothers above the age of 35 years is highest among the semi-urban Pandits, followed by the urban Pandits of Srinagar and least in the urban Pandits of Delhi.

Table 4.17

Distribution of births vis-a-vis age of mothers among the urban and the semi-urban Kashmiri Pandits and Muslims

Population	*Age at the time of birth of children*					
	19		*20-34*		*35+*	
	No.	*%*	*No.*	*%*	*No.*	*%*
Pandits						
Srinagar	80	15.66	408	80.29	23	4.5
Sopore	58	14.61	311	78.34	28	7.05
Delhi	35	11.15	277	88.21	2	0.64
Muslims						
Srinagar	124	17.37	547	76.51	43	6.02
Sopore	75	13.35	469	83.45	18	3.20

Among the Muslims the semi-urban population compared to the urban population has the higher percentage frequency of children born to women aged 20 to 34 years and least frequency of children born to women below the age of 20 years as well as above the age of 35 years.

Thus, it may be said that among the Pandits, the urban Pandits of Delhi have the greatest chances of having genetically healthier children (i.e. free from any chromosomal or other genetic disorders; because of the higher percentages of children born to

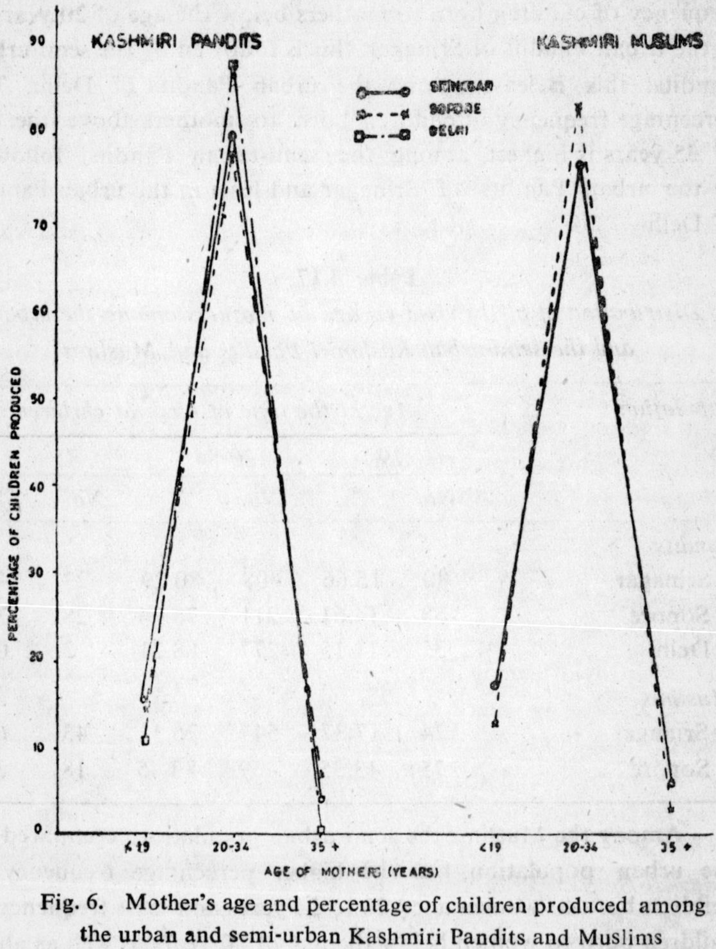

Fig. 6. Mother's age and percentage of children produced among the urban and semi-urban Kashmiri Pandits and Muslims

women aged 20-24 years and lower percentages of children born to women aged above 35 years and to women below 20 years of age) followed by the urban Pandits of Srinagar and least among the semi-urban Pandits. However, among the Muslims, the semi-urban population compared to the urban population, has the greater chances of having healthier children because of the higher percentages of children born to women aged 20-34 years and lower percentage of children born to women below 20 years of age and to women above 35 years of age.

III. Fertility Performance in relation to age of women at marriage:

Regarding fertility vis-a-vis age at marriage, the results obtained by Bhowmik et al (1971) are widely accepted. Accordingly, it is believed that women who are married earlier are endowed with higher fertility. With this hypothesis the study was carried out to find out the relationship between fertility performance and the age of women at marriage in the presently considered urban and semi-urban populations.

The results of effects of age at marriage on fertility performance have been set out in table (4.18). Though the differences in fertility performance are not significant either in urban or semi-urban populations of both the communities except among the urban Pandits of Srinagar, it is observed that there is a consistent trend that women marrying late tend to have lesser number of children than the women marring early. However, the differences were found to be statistically not significant.

The factors generally associated with fertility are many, and the age of women at marriage is only one of them; it is not easy to isolate the contribution of any one factor to the level of fertility. The relationship between age at marriage and fertility has been studied by many demographers but no consistent relationship has been demonstrated. Coale and Tye (1961) have come to the conclusion that postponement of marriage does contribute substantially to a reduction in birth rate and population growth. In the Mysore population studies (U.N. 1966) it was observed that females marrying between 14 and 17 years of age gave birth to 5.9

Table 4.18

Fertility Performance and Age of Mothers at Marriage among the Urban and semi-urban Kashmiri Pandits and Muslims

Population	*Age at Marriage in years*	*Women with children* *No.*	*Women with children* *%*	*Live Births* *No.*	*Live Births* *%*
Pandits					
Srinagar	Early (up to 15)	46	24.86	171	33.47
	Late (above 15)	139	75.14	3 0	66.53
	Total	185	100 00	511	100.C0
	Median = 15 years				
	X^2 = 4.0981, d.f. = 1, ·05>P> 02				
Sopore	Early (up to 17)	54	44.26	210	52.90
	Late (above 17)	68	55.74	187	47.10
	Total	122	100 00	397	100 00
	Median = 17 years				
	X^2 = 1.8064, d.f. = 1, .20>P>.10				
Delhi	Early (up to 18)	54	54.54	202	64.33
	Late (above 18)	45	45.46	112	35.67
	Total	99	100.00	314	100 00
	Median = 18 years				
	X^2 = 2.8455, d f. = 1, .10>P>.05				
Muslims					
Srinagar	Early (up to 15)	96	51.39	406	56 86
	Late (above 15)	89	48.11	308	43 14
	Total	185	100.00	417	100.00
	Median = 15 years				
	X^2 = 1.6903, d f. = 1, .20>P>.10				
Sopore	Early (up to 17)	68	45.95	286	50.89
	Late (above 17)	80	54.05	276	49.11
	Total	148	100.00	562	100.00
	Median = 17 years				
	X^2 = 0.9863, d.f. = 1, .50>P>.30				

children on an average while those marrying between 18 and 21 years gave birth to only 4.7 children. Agarwala (1964) and Goyal (1975) have shown that a reduction of about 16 to 50% is possible in birth rate if the marriage age of females is raised from 15 to 19-20 years. A comparative study of the Indian census figures has shown that there was an increase in the mean age at marriage for females from 13.67 in 1921 to 17.2 in 1971. The corresponding decrease in birth rate was from 46.4 in 1921-30 to 37.7 in 1969-70. According to Hans Raj (1978) the belief that in developed countries fertility is low because of late marriages, is not true as in USA and France marriages take place at younger ages. Yet the on going rise in the average age of women at marriage is expected to be a factor of considerable importance so far as India is concerned. In considering this, distinction is to be made between a girl's age at her wedding ceremony and at the beginning of her marital sexual relation. Even though the nuptial ceremony called Gauna, whereby the regular sexual relationship of the couple begins long after marriage is not prevalent among Kashmiris, the Pandits did have an identical custom which has almost died down with the passage of time both because of spread of education among girls and increase in the age at marriage. According to this custom the girls did not share the bed room of their husbands even after marriage for quite some time. This was allowed only after an auspicious day was fixed by the parents in mutual consultation and it was then that the marriage was consumated. The age at this juncture only would, therefore, have to be taken into account for the purpose of the study of the effect of age at marriage on fertility. This custom was found to have completely vanished among the migrant Pandits population of Delhi. At Srinagar the prevalence of this custom was found to be negligible and the number of such cases at Sopore was so low that it would not affect the conclusion any way.

From the tables 4.18 it is seen that the ratio of fertility between older and younger Pandit women is 135 : 89 at Srinagar 120 : 84 at Sopore and 118 : 78 at Delhi. In the case of Muslims the ratio is 110 : 90 at Srinagar and 111 : 91 at Sopore. This suggests that the effect of early marriage on fertility at Sopore is slightly less whereas at Delhi and Srinagar it is more pronounced. The present study, therefore, seems to support the general belief that younger age at marriage, both in urban and semi-urban populations of the two communities, is associated with higher fertility. Apparently this may be because of longer reproductive period of younger married women with a consequent increased vulnerability to conception. If the goal is to restrict the birth rate then there has to be a significant rise in the ages at marriage of women, for a small increase of a few years is not going to make any discernible dent on this rate; the reason being fecundity playing a vital role at the age interval of 15-20 years. According to a study conducted by Talwar (1965) 40% of married women were non-fecund at age 15. This rate gradually decreased to 29% at 16, 22% at 17 and 9% at 18 till the age of 19 when the non-fecundity of the female population came to nil. This means that the increase in the age at marriage has to be more than 5 years to show any significant results. Aggarwal (1966) does not, however, agree with this. He observes that the women in Kerala marry at about an average age of 20 and produce as many children as do Punjabi women who marry at an average of 17.5 years. But, for proper comparison it would be desirable to compare women belonging to the same socio-cultural group as has been done inthe present study.

IV. Fertility Performance and duration of interval between Marriage and '0' Parity

Another important factor closely related to the earlier factor, viz., age of females and marriage, is the duration of interval between marriage and '0' Parity. A shorter interval may expose a woman to a greater number of children. However, the age at marriage would obviously play an important role in determining this interval. Because of adolescent infertility a female would not develop into full reproductive maturity for several years after her first menstruation was set in. During this period, which may be any time between 13 years of age and 15-16 years, there are less chances of conception than at the age of 19 or 20 years.

So the woman whose sexual life begins soon after first menstruation are likely to have a longer average interval between marriage and '0' parity. Thus the effect of the interval on fertility is conditioned by the age of female at menstruation and marriage. It is generally accepted that the shorter is this interval, the longer is the reproductive span for a woman and consequently higher the fertility. With this in view a study of the relationship that might exist between the interval between marriage and '0' Parity and fertility was carried out on the urban and semi-urban Kashmiri Pandit and Muslim populations.

From table (4.19) it is observed that in both urban and semi-urban Pandits and Muslims there is a greater percentage of live births when the interval between age at marriage and 'O' parity is shorter than when it is longer. The differences found were, however, of no statistical significance.

When the interval between age at marriage and zero parity is short—the semi-urban Pandits have a higher percentage of children than that of urban Pandits of Delhi but a lower percentage of children than that of urban Pandits of Srinagar. When this interval is long, then the urban Pandits of Delhi have the highest percentage of children followed by that of semi-urban Pandits and the urban Pandits of Srinagar show the least percentage of live births.

Among the Muslims, the semi-urban have higher percentage of children when the interval is short than the urban and the opposite is true when the interval is long.

Thus it may be said that urban, semi-urban factor does not seem to play any decisive role in case of effect of interval between '0' parity and age at marriage on fertility.

V. Duration of Mrrried Life and Fertility

One of the most obvious and important factors affecting fertility is the length of period during which the couple remains together. This togetherness is temporarily affected by economic and social needs and permanently by natural (death) and emotional

Table 4.19

Fertility Performance and Interval between marriage and first child among the urban and semi-urban Kashmiri Pandits and Muslims

Population	*Interval (in years)*	*Women with children* No.	*Women with children* %	*Live Births* No.	*Live Births* %
Pandits					
Srinagar	Short (up to 3)	146	78.92	394	77.10
	Long (above 3)	39	21.08	117	22.90
	Total	185	100.00	511	100 00
	Median 3				
	$X^2 = 0.2119$, d.f. = 1, $.70 > P > .50$				
Sopore	Short (up to 3)	85	69.67	256	64.48
	Long (above 3)	37	30.33	141	35.52
	Total	122	100.00	397	100.00
	Median 3				
	$X^2 = 1.0281$, d.f. = 1, $.50 > P > .30$				
Delhi	Short (up to 3)	61	61.62	184	58 60
	Long (above 3)	38	38 38	130	41.40
	Total	99	100.00	314	100 00
	Median 3				
	$X^2 = .2049$, d.f. = 1, $.70 > P > .50$				
Muslims					
Srinagar	Short (up to 3)	147	79.46	550	77.03
	Long (above 3)	38	20.54	164	22.97
	Total	185	100.00	714	100.00
	Median 3				
	$X^2 = 0.1541$, d.f. = 1, $.70 > P > .50$				
Sopore	Short (up to 3)	113	76.35	454	80.78
	Long (above 3)	35	23.65	108	19.22
	Total	148	100.00	562	100.00
	Median 3				
	$X^2 = 1.0227$, d.f. = 1, $.50 > P > .30$				

(divorce) causes. For vocational exigencies the husband may have to live alone away from his spouse. Traditionally, the wife may be required to live with her parents and other relatives for various social customs. This temporary separation reduces the frequency of cohabitation and should affect the fertility. On the other hand the marriage may not turn out to be successful and due to emotional problems strained relations may lead to separation or even divorce. The imoprtant natural cause is the death of the spouse.. Since the earlier taboos against widow remarriage are no longer relevant, the period of widowhood and its effect on fertility depends on how soon the women decides to remarry. However, from the present data only the study of the relation between the duration of married life as a whole on fertility is feasible. The fertility performance of the women with shorter duration of married life, (up to the mean values) was compared with those with longer duration, (i.e., above the mean value). The hypothesis is that women having longer duration of married life should have more fertility.

Table (4.20) reveals that there is a uniform trend in both the semi-urban and the urban populations of both the communities that the women having longer duration of married life have higher fertility than the women who have shorter duration of married life. The variations observed were found to be significant in all except in the Delhi sample of urban Pandits where the difference was found to be statistically not significant. This may possibly be because of a much higher mean duration of marriage (25 years) as compared to 16 to 18 years in rest of the populations.

VI. Fertility in relation to level of literacy

Literacy level is an important characteristic of a population. Literacy was defined in the census of India as "the ability to both read and write in any language." Of the modern social factors that influence fertility, the education of girls is particularly relevant to family planning policies because increased public investment in it should bring about reduced fertility relatively quickly and with continuing effect. Table (4.21) gives

Table 4 20

Fertility Performance and duration af married life among the urban and semi-urban Kashmiri Pandits and Muslims

Population	*Duration af married life (in years)*	*Women with children*		*Live births*	
		No.	*%*	*No.*	*%*
Pandits					
Srinagar	Up to 18	99	53.51	202	39.53
	Above 18	86	46.49	309	60.47
	Total	185	100.00	511	100 00
	Median 18				
	$X^2 = 7.5782$, d.f. $= 1$, $.01>p>.001$				
Sopore	Up to 18	69	56.56	164	41.31
	Above 18	53	43.44	233	58.69
	Total	122	100.00	397	100.00
	Median 18				
	$X^2 = 6.4335$, d.f. $= 1$, $.10>p>.05$				
Delhi	Up to 25	40	40.40	94	29.94
	Above 25	59	59 60	220	70.06
	Total	99	100.00	314	100 00
	Median 25				
	$X^2 = 3.5974$, d.f. $= 1$, $.10>p>.05$				
Muslims					
Srinagar	Up to 16	119	64.32	350	49.02
	Above 16	66	35.68	364	50.98
	Total	185	100.00	714	100.00
	Median 16				
	$X^2 = 7.1281$, d.f. $= 1$, $.01>p>.001$				
Sopore	Up to 17	79	53.38	217	38.62
	Above 17	69	46.62	345	61.38
	Total	148	100.00	562	100.00
	Median 17				
	$X^2 = 7.7813$, d.f. $= 1$, $.01>p>.001$				

Table 4.21

Literacy Rate in India (1921-1981)

Year	*Males*	*Females*	*Total*
1921*	12.2	1.8	7.2
1931*	15.6	2.9	9.5
1941*	24.9	7.3	16.1
1951	24.9	7.9	16.7
1961	34.4	13.0	24.0
1971	39.5	18.7	24.5
1981	46.74	16.67	36.17

*For undivided India

Source : 1921-61—D. Natarajan (1972). 1971 and 81 Registrar General and Census Commissioner.

the literacy rate (Percentage of literates to total population) from 1921 to 1981 in India.

The States in India are divided into two categories, one those which show literacy rates higher than the all India average and the other which show lower rates. The state of Jammu & Kashmir falls under the second category. In 1971 census the J & K state showed literacy rates 18.6 (overall), 26.7 (Males) and 9.3 (Females) as against 11.0, 17.0 and 3.4, respectively in 1961. Thus there was an overall progress of 69 1% for men and 116.3% for women.

The relation between level of literacy and fertility has been a controversial topic particularly because of the belief that the fertility decline in the West has been caused at least in part by advances in education for the general population (Stycos, 1970).

The relevant surveys show that women who have attended high school have significantly fewer children than those with less education. The general tendency is for fertility to go down as the number of years in school goes up, a prominent exception being that women with only a little schooling have on an average more children than do the illiterate women. Perhaps this reflects the trend that those poor families who began to attain better nutrition and health resources increase their fertility for some time before taking on the higher status behaviour patterns that lower fertility (Datta 1961, Hawthorn 1970).

In Egypt, based on survey data from rural areas, Khalifa (1976) found an inverse relationship between wife's education and number of live births. That differential fertility by education does exist in India is indicated by such studies which have been carried out by United Nations (1966) in Bangalore city (1952), by Mukherjee and Singh (1961) in Bombay, by Driver (1963) in Central India by Ishrat Hussain (1972) in Lucknow and more recently by George (1976) in rural Kerala.

In the National Sample Survey round of 1960-61, (Mandelbaun, 1974), 16285 urban women aged 47 and above were interviewed and their responses were grouped according to six educational classes from illiterate to college and above. The average number of children born alive to women who had only primary schooling was 6.57, for those with a middle school education 5.04, and for matriculates it was 4.58. The sharpest decrease was between matriculates and those who had attended college education 2.01.

The report of the 1961-62 round (Mandelbaun, 1974) includes a rural sample of 32,453 women and an urban sample of 22,301 women. Both show a decrease in average number of children born alive with an increase in women's educational class above the primary level.

In the Mysore study, four categories of women's education were listed. Not much difference in fertility appeared among the city women in the categories up to 'High School or Universities'.

Driver's survey in Nagpur district set up three classes of women's education: None, Primary and above Primary School. Again there was a sharp decline in the highest category.

The survey taken of 4420 households in Lucknow city by Hussain (1972) reports general fertility rates by class of education. The tabulations show a steady decline in general fertility rate with increasing education, even from illiterate (163.89 per thousand) to the next category 'below Primary' (145.16) and through primary (102.04) secondary (96.20) and higher (63.38).

The affect of education on women, which in turn affects the fertility behaviour, can be studied in the following ways:

(*a*) An educated woman is usually less closely confined, physically and psychologically within her husband's family, and its narrow familial concerns, than is the woman who is brought into their home as an uneducated girl shortly after her menarche.

(*b*) The fact of her education as a girl is an index to the likelihood that the woman will marry into a family with enough resources. This will ensure better health conditions and reduce child-mortality to make her feel secure with lesser number of children. She will also be better able to tap varied resources in her time of need so that she is less totally dependent for safety on a large number of children.

(*c*) Girl's education is far more common today than it was in the past. A women may well be supported and reinforced in her inclination by educated kinfolk and friends. That is why an educated women today holds the motivations for smaller families more strongly and acts on them more effectively than did educated women of the older generation.

(*d*) Younger women who have attended high school since the start of the Indian Government's family planning compaign, know that family planning is feasible and desirable. The proportion of those who use modern contraceptive devices, therefore, rises steadily with increasing education.

(*e*) The higher the eduction for a woman the higher is her age at marriage. The rise in the age at marriage shortens the reproductive span of the woman while she is married and exposed to the risk of pregnancy (Vig, 1976). Cousequently lesser number of children are born.

(*f*) The education itself educates a woman about the adverse effects of having too many children - having too many children is associated with poor health of both mother and child and with poor child care which results in higher child mortality (Dasverma and Balasubramanian, 1976).

A demographic investigation was accordingly carried out on Kashmiri urban and semi-urban populations in order to have a comparable study of the correlation between the educational status of women with their fertility behaviour. 469 urban (284 Pandit and 185 Muslim) and 270 semi-urban (122 Pandit and 148 Muslims women have been studied for the purpose. The number of live births were recorded. The women were categorised into five educational levels on the basis of their formal educational qualification:

1. No formal education
2. Middle school level
3. Secondary school level
4. Graduate level
5. Post-graduate and above level.

The fertility performance in educational level was measured as the average number of live births per marriage. The results are given in the table 4 22.

It is seen from this table that the average number of live births per marriage decreases with the increase in the level of education both among the urban and the semi-urban populations. However, among the semi-urban Muslims the average number of live births per marriage is lowest at the middle School education level. This may be due to chance fluctuation. The decline in the average number of children per marriage is maximum from women with no formal educations to women with Middle School education both among the urban and the semi-urban Pandits and the Muslims.

Thus among the urban and the semi-urban Padits and the Muslims, the population growth may be arrested by improving the literacy level to secondary school level and above.

VII. Sex of the Child and Fertility

In many Indian socio-cultural groups it is believed that children are the real possession of family. They are the source of

Table 4.22

Fertility vis-a-vis level of Literacy among the urban and the semi-urban Kashmiri Pandits and Muslims

Population	*Education level*	*No. of women*	*%*	*Average number of live born children per marriage*
Pandits				
Srinagar	No formal education	36	19.46	3.83
	Middle	30	16.22	3.20
	Secondary School	56	30.27	2.55
	Graduate	46	24.86	1.47
	Post-graduate	17	9.19	1.44
Sopore	No formal education	55	45.08	3.99
	Middle	14	11.48	2.78
	Secondary School	31	25.41	2.41
	Graduate	19	15.57	1.68
	Post-graduate	3	2.46	1.66
Delhi	No formal education	24	24.24	4.42
	Middle	15	15.15	3.26
	Secondary School	26	26.26	3.11
	Graduate	22	22.22	2.04
	Post-graduate	12	12.12	1.50
Muslims				
Srinagar	No formal education	124	67.02	4.02
	Middle	28	15.14	2.82
	Secondary School	15	8.11	2.73
	Graduate	3	1.62	2.67
	Post-Graduate	15	8.11	1.8
Sopore	No formal education	115	77.70	3.93
	Middle	10	6.76	1.43
	Secondary School	15	10.14	1.53
	Graduate	6	4.05	1.8
	Post-graduate	2	1.35	1.5

strength and power for the parents. More particularly it is believed that with the help of male children alone the family can pull on and parental line can continue to exist. In such societies every effort is made to have male children and if the first and/or second child is a girl, the procreation may invariably be continued till a male child is born. Often such an attitude to child's sex is because of religious beliefs as well. A study was, therefore, carried out to make a comparison of the effect on fertility, if any, of such attitude between urban and semi-urban populations of Kashmiri Pandits and Muslims, respectively.

From table 4.23 it is observed that both urban and semi-urban Pandits show consistently larger family size in case of first two live borns being females than in case of first two live borns being males. But statistically no significant differences were found. No particular trend was observed among either the semi-urban or the urban muslim populations. It thus appears that preference for sex at '0' and first parity does not have any significant effect on the family size in either the semi-urban or urban populations of Pandits and Muslims respectively.

VII. Pregnancy Wastage and Fertility

Biologically, pregnancy wastage like abortions and miscarriages have adverse effect on fertility performance but once the biological factors are taken care of, psychologically it may have quite the opposite effect. A woman who gets abortion at the first and/or second conception, may tend to have more number of children for fear of losing them or vice versa—she may be afraid of having more children because of the unpleasant experiences associated with the pregnancy wastages. Latter seems to hold true in case of present study as revealed by the table (4.24). It is observed that in both—urban and the semi-urban population samples of Pandits and Muslims, the family tends to be larger when no pre-natal deaths have occured at first and/or second conception. But statistically the difference was found to be not significant.

Table 4.23

Sex of the first and second child vis-a-vis Family size among the urban and the semi-urban Kashmiri Pandits and Muslims

Population	*Sex of the 1st & 2nd child*	*No. of women*	*No. of children*	*Family size in terms of Av. No. of children per family*
Pandits				
Srinagar	Both male	49	120	2.45
	1st male 2nd female	47	125	2.66
	1st female 2nd male	47	117	2.49
	Both female	42	124	2.95
Sopore	Both male	25	82	3.28
	1st male 2nd female	40	110	2.75
	1st female 2nd male	31	87	2.81
	Both female	26	91	3.50
Delhi	Both male	26	66	2.54
	1st male 2nd female	26	76	2.92
	1st female 2nd male	24	77	3.21
	Both female	23	60	3.48
Muslims				
Srinagar	Both male	57	189	3.32
	1st male 2nd female	52	177	3.40
	1st female 2nd male	26	95	3.65
	Both female	53	192	3.62
Sopore	Both male	41	135	3.29
	1st male 2nd female	37	103	2.78
	1st female 2nd male	28	111	3.96
	Both female	42	154	3.67

IX. Infant Mortality and Fertility Performance

Another factor that affects and influences fertility is infant mortality which was very high in the past. Accordingly the fertility was high to compensate for the possible deaths. Today the society has controlled many diseases which were fatal in the case of children. Even then it was considered feasible to study the effect of this factor particularly because the mortality rates of urban and semi-urban areas differ and so do the attitude to family size.

Results of effect of infant mortality suffered at 1st and/or 2nd Parity on family size, have been set out in table (4.25). Though the differences in family size are statisitcally not significant be it urban or semi-urban populations of both the communities, yet there is a consistent trend that women having suffered infant deaths at 1st and/or 2nd parity have lesser number of children than the women who have had no such experience at the first two conceptions.

Table 4.24

Pre-natal deaths at 1st and/or 2nd conception vis-a-vis Family size among urban Kashmiri Pandits and Muslims

Population	*Any Pre-Natal deaths suffered at 1st and/or 2nd conception*	*No of women*	*No. of children*	*Family size*
Pandits				
Srinagar	Yes	6	13	2.17
	No	179	473	2.64
Sopore	Yes	5	12	2.4
	No	117	358	3.05
Delhi	Yes	9	24	2.67
	No	90	275	3.05
Muslims				
Srinagar	Yes	6	15	2.5
	No	179	638	3 56
Sopore	Yes	4	11	2.75
	No	144	492	3.42

Table 4.25

Infant Mortality at '0' and/or 1st Parity vis-a-vis Family Size among the urban and the semi-urban Kashmiri Pandit and Muslim

Population	*Infant mortality (below 1 yr. of age) suffered*	*No. of women*	*No. of children*	*Family size*
Pandits				
Srinagar	Yes	12	24	2.0
	No	173	462	2.67
Sopore	Yes	7	18	2.57
	No	115	352	3.06
Delhi	Yes	8	19	2.38
	No	91	280	3.08
Muslims				
Srinagar	Yes	21	72	3.43
	No	164	581	3.54
Sopore	Yes	24	76	3.17
	No	124	427	3.44

Growth Rate of Family Sizes

After studying the effects of various bio-social factors on fertility of the urban and semi-urban samples of Kashmiri Pandit and Muslim populations it is necessary to gauge the net increase in the family size to see the trend in growth rate, and make a comparison of this rate *vis-a-vis* urban and semi-urban populations. These rates have been set out in table 4.26.

The pattern of growth rate that emerges from figure (7) indicates that this rate has been greater among the semi-urban Pandits than among the urban Pandits.

Further, the urban Pandits of Srinagar show steeper rise than the migrant urban Pandits of Delhi.

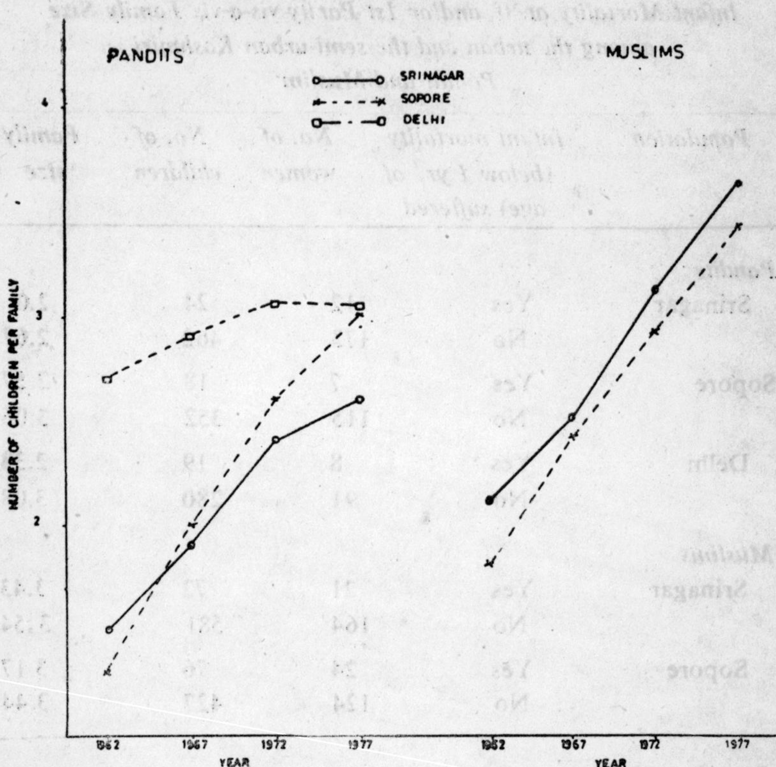

Fig 7. Growth rate of family size among the urban and semi-urban Kashmiri Pandits and Muslims

Table 4.26
Growth Rate vis-a-vis Family Size among the urban and the semi-urban Kashmiri Pandits and Muslims

Population	*Number of children per family in the years*			
	1962	*1967*	*1972*	*1977*
Pandits				
Srinagar	1.50 (.38)	1.88 (.51)	2.39 (.24)	2.63
Sopore	1.29 (.68)	1.97 (.59)	2.56 (.47)	3.03
Delhi	2.70 (.29)	2.89 (.16)	3.05 (—.03)	3.02
Muslims				
Srinagar	2.07 (.43)	2.50 (.63)	3.13 (.43)	3.56
Sopore	1.81 (.55)	2.36 (.50)	2.86 (.54)	3.40

Similarly among the Kashmiri Muslims, the semi-urban Muslims seem to have greater growth rate than the urban muslims.

It may, therefore, be inferred that the cumulative effect of bio-social demographic factors including the impact of birth control measures seems to be greater in the urban Pandits and Muslims populations than their semi-urban counterparts. Further, the migrant urban Pandits of Delhi have experienced greater impact of such (bio-social demographic) factors than the urban Pandits of Srinagar and they have registered a minus growth rate between 1972 and 1977 (—0.03).

CHAPTER

5

Differences Between Kashmiri Pandits and Kashmiri Muslims Fertility and Mortality

IN THIS CHAPTER the same methods for estimating fertility as stated by Barclay and as adopted in the previous Chapter have been adopted. While in the previous chapter the urban and semi-urban variations in fertility have been examined, this chapter has been designed to analyse the inter population variation in fertility between Pandits and Muslims both at Srinagar and Sopore.

Child-woman Ratio

The ratio of children in the age interval 0-4 years to every 1000 women of Kashmiri Pandits in comparison to that of Kashmiri Muslims is given in table 5.1.

The child-woman ratio of Muslims is observed to be higher than that of Pandits at both the places. Though, however, there is no significant difference in the child-women ratio between Pandits and Muslims at Sapore ($X^2=0.56$), the child woman ratio of Muslims significantly higher than that of Kashmiri Pandits at Srinagar ($X^2=7.21$).

Crude Birth Rate

From Table 5.2 it is seen that the crude Birth Rate in respect of Pandits is lower than that of Muslims. The difference, however,

Table 5.1

Child-woman ratio among the Kashmiri Pandits and Kashmiri Muslims of Srinagar and Sopore

Population	*No. of children (0-4 year)*	*No. of women (15-19 years)*	*Child-woman Ratio*
Srinagar			
Pandits	43	161	267.1
Muslims	81	170	476.5
Sopore			
Pandits	55	101	544.5
Muslims	81	126	642.5

Table 5.2

Crude Birth Rates among the Kashmiri Pandits and Muslims of Srinagar and Sopore

Population	*No. of live births*	*No. of total population*	*Crude Birth Rate*
Srinagar			
Pandits	9	638	14.11
Muslims	21	1020	20.58
Sopore			
Pandits	14	606	23.10
Muslims	30	882	34.01

is non-significant at both the places (X^2 being 0.92 and 1.45 respectively). The estimated Crude Birth Rate for all India was 38 in 1971 which reduced to 33 in 1978. Thus the Crude Birth rate revealed by the present study of Pandits and Muslims is less than the national figure except in the case of Muslims at Sopore in whose case it is slightly higher (34.01).

Even though this rate is an adequate measure of fertility when comparing populations of different levels, yet this is not considered scientific as this rate at any given time is the result of inter action of three different factors viz., the level of fertility, the age structure of the population (particularly that of the female component) and the age distribution of fertility.

General Fertility Rate (G.F.R.)

Although the General Fertility Rate gives a much better account than the Crude Birth Rate, it has its own drawbacks. It does not take into account the specific age composition of the women in the child-bearing age as such. Any two populations with exactly, the same G.F.R. may differ considerably in the specific age group depending upon the proportion of women in each group. Hence it is also not an adequate measure of fertility.

Table 5.3 gives the General Fertility Rates of Kashmiri Pandits and Muslims.

Table 5.3

General Fertility Rates among the Kashmiri Pandits and Muslims of Srinagar and Sopore

Population	*No. of live Births*	*No. of women 15-49 years*	*G.F.R.*
Srinagar			
Pandits	9	161	55.9
Muslims	21	170	123.53
Sopore			
Pandits	14	101	138.61
Muslims	30	126	238.1

It is seen that the General Fertility Rate of Muslims is higher than that of Pandits of both urban and semi-urban places. The difference is significant at Srinagar ($X^2=3.96$) but non-significant at Sopore ($X^2=2.47$). We also observe that the G.F.R. in respect of Pandits of urban and semi-urban areas and of Muslims of urban areas is lower than all India rate of 1972 (Fertility Differentials in India—Vital Statistics Division, Registrar General and Census Commissioner). In the case of Pandits it is 55.9 and 138.61 as against all India figure of 131.4 and 171.1. For Muslims it is 138.61 against all India 150.8. However in the case of Sopore Muslims the G.F.R. is much higher 238.1 against the all India rate for rural Muslim of 191.5.

According to 1969 sample Registration Survey for rural India (Agarwala, 1973) General Fertility Rate was found to be 174.1. Thus it will be seen that the General Fertility Rate of Muslims is higher than this rate at both the places while that of Pandits is less.

Age-Specific Fertility Rate

To meet the shortcoming of the General Fertility Rate explained in the previous para, Age-specific Birth Rates of Kashmiri Pandits *vis-a-vis* Muslims has been analysed vide Table 5.4.

Table 5.4

Age-specific Birth Rates among the Kashmiri Pandits and Muslims of Srinagar and Sopore

Populatian	*15-19*	*20-24*	*25-29*	*30-34*	*35-39*	*40-44*	*45-49*
Srinagar							
Pandits	0	400.00	90.90	0	0	0	0
Muslims	333.33	500.00	97.56	56.6	90.91	0	71.43
Sopore							
Pandits	0	375.00	259.25	148.14	0	0	0
Muslims	333.33	588.23	413.79	304.34	0	0	0

According to the National Sample Survey (1963) and All India Census (1971) the Indian fertility is of an 'Early peak type' for an Indian women reaches the peak of fertility in the age group of 20-24. This is true of Pandits and Muslims of Kashmir both urban and semi-urban (Figure 8). At Srinagar the Pandit woman shows fertility in the age span of 20-29 only whereas the fertility of Muslim women spreads over the entire span of 15 to 49 years. In the case of semi-urban population of Sopore the fertility span of Kashmiri Pandits is from 20 to 34 whereas that of Muslims it is 15 to 34. However, because of the fact that in both Pandits and Muslims of Srinagar and Sopore, the maximum number of children are born to women in the age group 20-24 yrs, any child with congenital malformation which bears any relation to mother's age (mothers of less than 20 years of age and above 34 years of age) is not likely to be produced, neither in Pandits nor in Muslims.

Thus Kashmiris, irrespective of whether they are Pandits or Muslims, may be under low genetic load leading to more viability of their children.

Total Fertility Rates

Table 5.5 gives the Total Fertility rates in respect of Kashmiri Pandits of Srinagar and Sopore *vis-a-vis* Muslims at these places.

Table 5.5

Total Fertility Rates among the Kashmiri Pandits and Muslims of Srinagar and Sopore

Population	*Total Fertility Rate*	*No. of children per woman*
Srinagar		
Pandits	2454.5	2.45
Muslims	5749.15	5.75
Sopore		
Pandits	3911.9	3.91
Muslims	8198.5	8.20

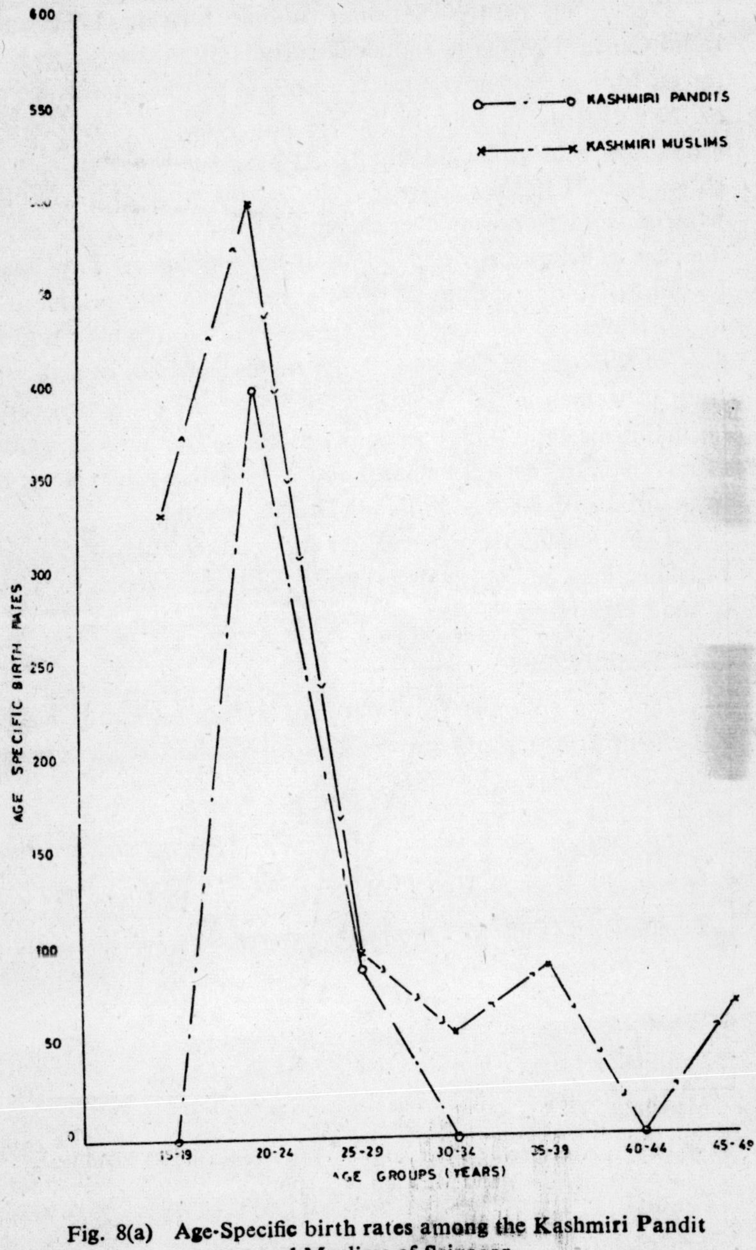

Fig. 8(a) Age-Specific birth rates among the Kashmiri Pandit and Muslims of Srinagar

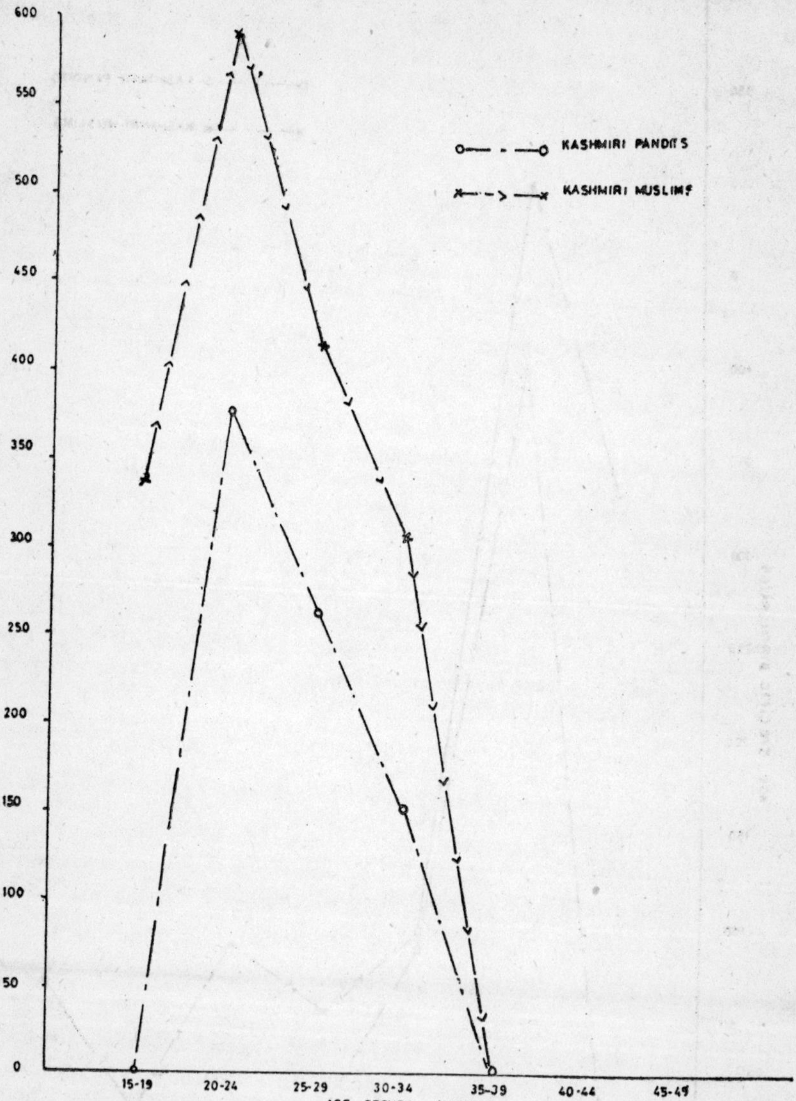

Fig. 8(b) Age specific birth rates among the Kashmiri Pandits and Muslims of Sopore

It is seen that total fertility rate of Muslims is higher than that of Kashmiri Pandits both at Srinagar and Sopore. The total fertiliity rate of Kashmiri Pandits of Srinagar and Sopore is less than all India rate of 1972 (4.2 for urban and 5.7 for rural) but the rate in respect of Muslims is higher than all India rate of 4.9 (urban) and 6.2 (rural).

Therefore, it may be inferred that in Srinagar, while the Pandit population is eventually likely to become stable, the Muslim population is growing almost three times that of Pandits.

However in Sopore, the Muslims are growing only about two times that of Pandits.

Cumulative Natality Rate

Table 5.6 gives the Cumulative Natality rate of Kashmiri Pandits and Muslim at urban Srinagar and semi-urban Sopore and compares their respective rate.

A study of the table 5.6 shows that there is no stability in the cumulative Natality Rate of Muslims at Srinagar whereas in the case of Pandits the CNR stabilises from the age interval of 25-29. In contrast the CNR of both Pandits and Muslims at Sopore shows stability from the age interval of 30-34.

Gross Reproduction Rate

Gross Reproduction rate shows how many girl babies—The potential future mothers—would be born to 1000 women passing through their child bearing years, if the age-specific birth rate of a given year remained constant and if no woman entering the child bearing period died before reaching the menopause age. From table 5.7 we see that Pandits have GRR of less than 1000 and Muslims have more than 1000. Therefore Muslims have more daughters born to them than Pandits in Srinagar as well as in Sopore.

Consequently, the Pandit populations at both Srinagar and Sopore under the threat of being reduced in size because of the future deficiency of females in the reproductive age group.

Table 5.6

Cumulative Natality Rates among the Kashmiri Pandits and Muslims of Srinagar and Sopore

Populations	*Age groups*						
	15-19	*20-24*	*25-29*	*30-34*	*35-39*	*40-44*	*45-49*
Srinagar							
Pandits	0	2000	2454.50	2454.50	2454.50	2454.50	2454.50
Muslims	1666.65	4166.65	4654.45	4937.45	5392.0	5392.0	5749.15
Sopore							
Pandits	0	1875	3171.25	3911.95	3911.95	3911.95	3911.95
Muslims	1666.65	4607.8	6676.75	8198.45	8198.45	8198.45	8198.45

Table 5.7

Gross Reproduction Rates among the Kashmiri Pandits and Muslims of Srinagar and Sopore

Population	G.R.R.
Srinagar	
Pandits	818.16
Muslims	1642.61
Sopore	
Pandits	838.28
Muslims	4099.22

But reverse is true in case of Muslim population of these places, who are imposing the threat of population explosion due to a significant increase in the number of future mothers.

However, genetically speaking, there is a likelihood of decrease in the frequency of X-linked recessive lethal genes in the Pandits of both, Srinagar and Sopore while there are more chances of increase in such genes among the Muslims of Srinagar as well as of Sopore.

Age at Menarche and at Menopause

With the onset of menstruation (i.e. menarche) women assume fertility and the cessation of menstrual flow is known as menopause. The span between menarche and menopause is the reproductive period of a woman and pregnancy can occur at any time during this period.

Age at Menarche

From the table [5.8(a)], it is observed that the highest frequency of women of, both Pandits and Muslims of Srinagar and Sopore is found in the age group of 14 years, followed by those in age-group 15 and 13 years, respectively for Pandits and Muslims.

Also, from table [5.8(b)], it is seen that the mean age at menarche is slightly higher in Pandits than in Muslims, at Srinagar (higher by 0.18) and Sopore (higher by 0.48).

Table 5.8(a)

Percentage distribution of women by the age at menarche in Pandits and Muslims of Srinagar and Sopore

Population	*Age at menarche*								
	11	*12*	*13*	*14*	*15*	*16*	*17*	*18*	*19*
Srinagar									
Pandits	3.24	10.8	15.7	33.0	30.3	5.4	0.54	0.54	0.54
Muslims	2.16	10.27	27.57	34.59	15.67	8.65	0.54	0.54	—
Sopore									
Pandits	0.82	7.4	13.9	40.2	22.1	11.5	2.5	0	1.64
Muslims	2.03	12.16	23.65	37.84	18.24	3.38	1.35	0.67	0.67

Table 5.8(b)

Mean age at Menarche among the Kashmiri Pandits and Muslims of Srinagar and Sopore

Population	*Age at menarche*		
	Mean	*S. D.*	*S. E.*
Srinagar			
Pandits	14.01	1.29	0.09
Muslims	13.82	1.22	0.09
Sopore			
Pandits	14.29	1.32	0.12
Muslims	13.81	1.20	0.10

Age at Menopause

From Table (5.9) it is observed that in Srinagar, though the percentage distribution of women in both Pandits and Muslims, is highest in the 49-50 years age group, the mean age at menopause is slightly higher in Muslims (48.5) than in Pandits (47.31).

However, in Sopore, the Pandits and Muslims differ with respect to both, distribution as well as mean age at menopause.

Pandits have the maximum frequency of women in the 49-50 years age group, while Muslims have in the next age group in the 51-52 years age group.

Also, Muslims of Sopore have much higher mean age at menopause (49.9 years) than the Pandits (47 8 years).

Therefore, it may be inferred that Pandits and Muslims may or may not differ in the distribution but they do differ with respect to age at menopause, irrespective of whether they belong to Srinagar or Sopore.

Length of Reproductive Period

The length of reproductive period estimated from the mean age at menarche and mean age at menopause, disclose that in Srinagar, the Muslims have longer reproductive period (34.7 yrs.) than the Pandits (33.3 years).

Table 5.9(a)

Percentage distribution of women by the age at menopause in Pandits and Mnslims of Srinagar and Sopore

Population	*Age at Menopause*								
	<40	*41-42*	*43-44*	*45-46*	*47-48*	*49-50*	*51-52*	*53-54*	*55+*
Srinagar									
Pandits	6.45	6.45	3.23	22.58	19.35	29.03	6.45	3.23	3.23
Muslims	3.85	3.85	7.69	11.54	19.23	23.08	15.37	11.54	3.85
Sopore									
Pandits	4.17	8.33	4.17	16.67	20.83	29.17	4.17	4.17	8.32
Muslims	—	6.90	3.45	6.9	6.9	24.14	34.48	6.9	10.33

Table 5.9 (b)

Mean age at menopause among the Kashmiri Pandits and the Muslims

Population	Age at menopause		
	Mean	*S.D.*	*S.E.*
Srinagar			
Pandits	47.31	3.64	0.65
Muslims	48.5	3.81	0.75
Sopore			
Pandits	47.83	3.95	0.81
Muslims	49.9	3.62	0.67

Similarly, in Sopore also the Muslims have longer fertility period (36.1 years) than the Pandits (33.54 years).

Thus it appears that the Pandits and Muslims do vary with respect to length of reproductive period, at Srinagar and Sopore.

So, it may be concluded that greater population threat seems to come from Muslims than the Pandits at Srinagar and Sopore too because of the longer reproductive period in the case of Muslims.

Conceptions : Table 5.10 shows the results of conceptions of Kashmiri Pandit and Muslim samples. Total conception in respect of Kashmiri Pandits was 587 (Average 3.17) at Srinagar as against 786 (av. 4.25) for Muslims. At Sopore total conception was 444 (av. 3.64) among Pandits and 629 (av. 4.25) among Muslims. The average numbers of conceptions is higher in the case of Muslims at both the places being 4.25 but the variation is larger at Srinagar than at Sopore.

Mortality : Since the net increase in the population is the result of interaction of fertility and mortality, it is necessary to study the position of pre-natal and post-natal dgaths.

Table 5.10

Conceptions and Conception wastage among the Kashmiri Pandits and Muslims of Srinagar and Sopore

Population	Total No. of women	Total concep-tions	Average No. of concep-tions	Number of						
				Living children	Dead before 20 yrs. of age	Abortions		Mis-carriage	Still births	Preg-nancy
						Induced	Spon-taneous			
Srinagar										
Pandits	185	587	3.17	486 (82.79)	25 (4.26)	5 (0.85)	58 (9.88)	6 (1.02)	1 (0.17)	6 (1.02)
Muslims	185	786	4.25	653 (83.08)	61 (7.76)	0	50 (6.36)	18 (2.29)	2 (0.25)	2 (0.25)
Sopore										
Pandits	122	444	3.64	370 (83.33)	27 (6.08)	2 (0.45)	23 (5.18)	11 (2.48)	2 (2.45)	9 (2 02)
Muslims	148	629	4.25	503 (79.97)	59 (9.38)	0	45 (7.15)	14 (2.23)	5 (0 79)	3 (0 48)

Note : Figures in braackets show percentages

The three tables 5.11, 5.12 and 5.13 give the distribution of pre-natal deaths, and live borns between the two communities at Srinagar and Sopore. For purposes of pre-natal deaths, miscarriage, still births and spontaneous abortions have been taken into account.

Table 5.I1

Distribution of Pre-natal deaths, Post-natal deaths and Living children among the Kashmiri Pandits and Muslims of Srinagar and Sopore

Population	*Pre-Natal deaths*		*Post-Natal deaths*		*Living children*		χ^2
	No.	*%*	*No.*	*%*	*No.*	*%*	
Srinagar							
Pandits	65	11.07	25	4.26	486	81.09	36, d.f.=2.8
Muslims	70	8.91	61	7.76	653	83.08	.02>p>.01
Sopore							
Pandits	36	8.11	27	6.08	370	86.26	5.11, d.f.=2
Muslims	64	10.27	59	9.38	503	79.97	.10>p>.05

Table 5.12

Distribution of Pre-natal deaths and Live borns among the Kashmiri Pandits and Muslims of Srinagar and Sopore

Population	*Pre-natal deaths*		*Live borns*		χ^2
	No.	*%*	*No.*	*%*	
Srinagar					
Pandits	65	11.07	511	87.05	2.1. d.f.=1
Muslims	70	8.91	714	90.84	.20>p>.10
Sopore					
Pandits	36	8.11	397	89.41	1.10, d.f.=1
Muslims	64	10.27	562	89.35	.30>p>.20

Table 5.13

Distribution of Post-natal deaths and Live borns among the Kashmiri Pandits and Muslims of Srinagar and Sopore

Population	Post-natal deaths		Live borns		χ^2
	No.	%	No.	%	
Srinagar					
Pandits	25	4.26	511	87.05	5.44, d.f.=1
Muslims	61	7.76	714	90.84	$0.02>p>.01$
Sopore					
Pandits	27	6.08	397	89.41	3.37, d.f.=1
Muslims	59	9.38	562	89.35	$.10>p>.05$

It is observed that in Srinagar Muslim population sample shows a higher percentage of post natal deaths but a lower percentage of pre-natal deaths than that of Pandit population sample, while at Sopore the Muslims show a higher percentage of pre-natal deaths as well as of post-natal deaths than that in Pandits. Difference in post natal deaths is significant at Srinagar (X^2=5.44). The differences at Sopore (X^2=3.37) and differences in pre-natal deaths at Srinagar (X^2=3.48) and Sopore (X^2=0.661) are not found statistically significant. Therefore it may be said that there is a more intense post-natal selection among the Muslims than among Pandits at Srinagar.

Inter Population Comparisons

Table 5.14 gives a comparison of various fertility and mortality indices among various populations.

It is observed that the Pandits of Srinagar and Sopore have a lower child birth index, survival index and child loss index, respectively than their Muslim counterparts. This shows a greater pre-natal selection among the Pandits than the Muslims. However, post-natal selection seems to be more intense among the Muslims of Srinagar and Sopore than the Pandits.

Table 5.14

Fertility and Mortality Indices among the Kashmiri Pandits and Muslims of Srinagar and Sopore

Population	*Child Birth*	*Survival*	*Child Loss*	*Abortion rate/100*	*Miscarriage rate/100*	*Still Birth rate/100*
Srinagar						
Pandits	2.76	2.63	0.14	9.88	1.02	0.17
Muslims	3.86	3.53	0.30	6.36	2.29	0.25
Sopore						
Pandits	3.25	3.03	0.22	5.18	2.48	0.45
Muslims	3.80	3.40	0.40	7.15	2.23	0.79
Kanpur Muslims (Majumdar, 1960)	4.23	2.57	1.66	—	—	—
East Nimar, Muslims (Tiwari, 1974)	5.1	4.23	0.95	—	—	—
Mehrauli (Neeti, Buniyas, 77)	4.3	3.68	0.61	6.48	4.59	0.27

Bio-Social Factors. The bio-social factors which affect fertility have been discussed at length in Chapter IV. The various important studies carried out in this direction and the conclusions arrived at have also been briefly mentioned therein. Some of the factors taken up for examination in the present study have also been discussed in that Chapter. In this Chapter an attempt will be made to bring out a comparative study of the effects of these factors on the fertility of Kashmiri Pandit women of Srinagar and Sopore *vis-a-vis* the Muslim women of these places.

I. Mother's age—Parity and Frequency of Children

An attempt has been made to assess the distribution of mean age of mothers by the order of birth or parity and variance in the percentage of children produced according to the age of mothers at the time of birth of child, separately for Pandits and Muslims. The comparative results of the study are tabulated in Table 5.15.

Table 5.15

Mean age of mother at different parities among the Kashmiri Pandits and the Muslims of Srinagar and Sopore

Parity	*Mean age of Mothers at the time of Birth of children in years*			
	Srinagar		*Sopore*	
	Pandits	*Muslims*	*Pandits*	*Muslims*
0	20.96	21.37	21.02	20.67
I	23.79	22.17	23.68	23.71
II	25.72	24.26	26.20	24.89
III	28.89	26.90	29.04	27.54
IV	32.42	29.20	31.31	29.30
V	37.40	32.60	33.81	30.58
VI	39.50	33.12	38.6	31.30
VII	44	35.20	—	35.66

From the table 5.15 and the figure (9) it is seen that there is a steady but steep rise in the mean age of mothers from zero to higher parity in the case of Pandits at both the places. As regards Muslims that rise, though steady is comparatively less steeper. The mean age at '0' parity in the case of both Pandits and Muslims is around 21 years. Up to parity I, II, and III the increase in the mean age of Pandit mothers is almost uniform whereas in the case of Muslims it is almost uniform up to and including parity IV. The gap in the mean age of Pandits at Parity IV widens and is widest at Parity V. The mean age at zero parity shows that neither population has the threat of having such abnormalities as are common in children of younger mothers (Roy and Ghosh, 1972). Kashmiri Pandit mothers cross 34 years of age after 4th and 5th parity at Srinagar and Sopore whereas Muslim mothers cross it after 6th parity which shows that Muslims reach the risk of having children with a variety of congenital defects later than Kashmiri Pandits.

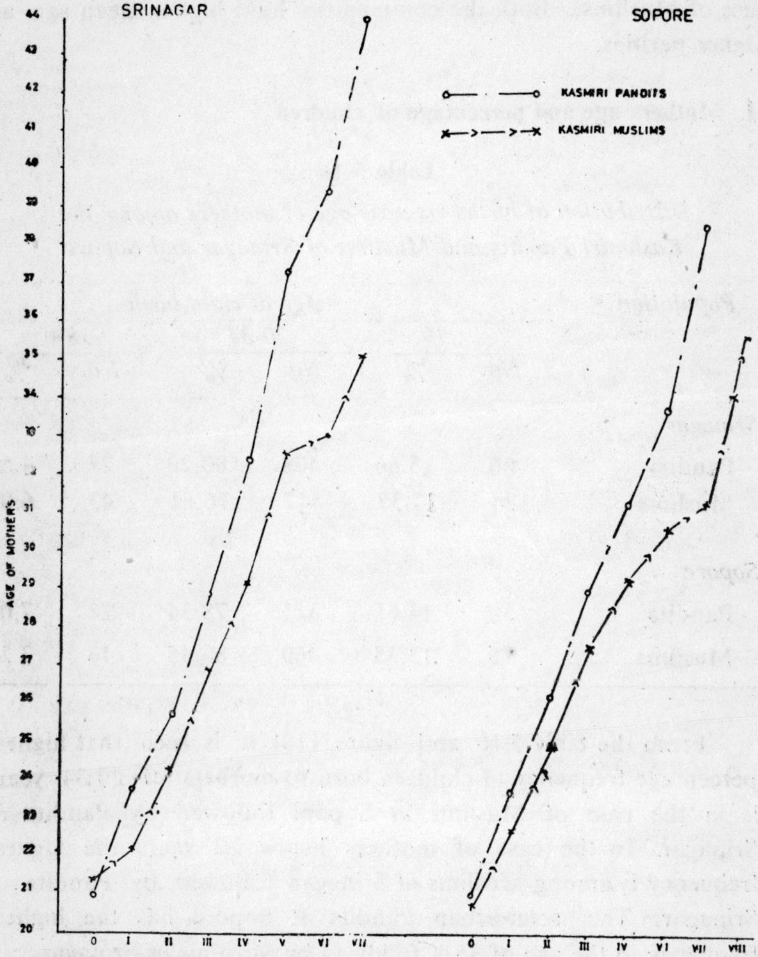

Fig. 9. Mother's age and parity among Kashmiri Pandits and Muslims

From a close look at the mean ages at Pandit and Muslim mothers it is seen that on an average there is a gap of 3 years between two births in the case of Pandits and only 2 years in the case of Muslims. Both the communities have higher mean age at higher parities.

II. Mothers age and percentage of children

Table 5.16

Distribution of births vis-a-vis age of mothers among the Kashmiri Pandits and Muslims of Srinagar and Sopore

Population	*Age at child birth*					
	<19		*20-34*		*35+*	
	No.	*%*	*No.*	*%*	*No.*	*%*
Srinagar						
Pandits	80	15.66	408	80.29	23	4.50
Muslims	124	17.37	547	76.61	43	6.02
Sopore						
Pandits	58	14.61	311	78.34	28	7.05
Muslims	75	13.35	469	83.45	18	3.20

From the table 5.16 and figure (10) it is seen that highest percentage frequency of childern born to mothers of 20-34 years is in the case of Muslims at Sopore followed by Pandits at Srinagar. In the case of mothers below 20 years the highest frequency is among Muslims of Srinagar followed by Pandits of Srinagar. The semi-urban Pandits at Sopore has the highest frequency in the age of 35+ followed by Muslims of Srinagar.

It is significant to note that the percentage frequency of children born to Muslim mothers below 19 years and above 34 years is the least at semi-urban Sopore.

Thus it may be concluded that among the urban samples Pandits have greater chances of having children free from any

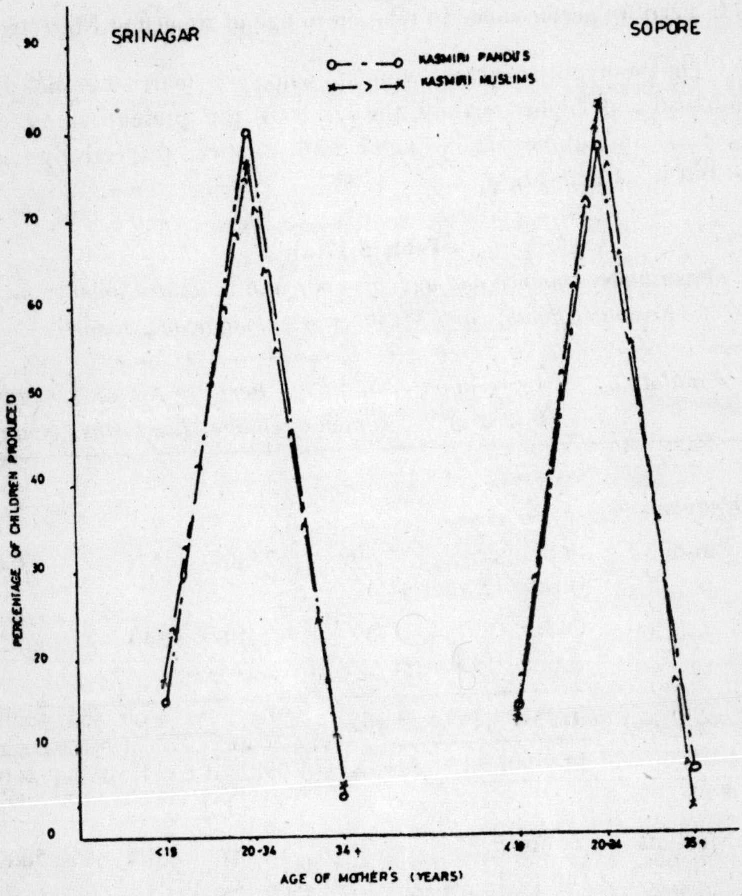

Fig. 10. Mother's age and percentage of children produced among the Kashmiri Pandits and Muslims

chromosomal or other genetic disorders whereas among the semi-urban samples Muslims have this advantage because of higher percentage of children born to mothers in the age group 20-34.

III. Fertility performance in relation to age of women at Marriage

On the hypothesis that women who are married earlier are endowed with higher fertility, the result of the present study on the two communities at Srinagar and Sopore, respectively, are set out in table 5.17.

Table 5.17(a)

Fertility performance and age of women at marriage among the Kashmiri Pandits and Muslims of Srinagar and Sopore

Population	*Age-group (in years)*	*No. of women*	*Per-centage*	*No. of live births*	*Per-centage*
Srinagar					
Pandits	Younger (up to 15 years)	46	24.86	171	33.47
	Older (above 15 years)	139	75.14	340	66.53
	Total	185		511	
	Median=15 years $X^2=4.0981$, d.f.=1, .05>P>.02				
Muslims	Younger (up to 15 years)	96	51.89	406	56.86
	Older (above 15 years)	89	48.11	308	43.14
	Total	185		714	
	Median=15 years $X^2=1.6903$. d.f.=1, .20>P>.10				

Table 5.17(b)

Population	*Age-group (in years)*	*No. of women*	*Per-centage*	*No. of women*	*Per-centage*
Sopore					
Pandits	Younger (up to 17 years)	54	44.26	210	52.90
	Older (above 17 years)	68	54.74	187	47.10
	Total	122		397	
	Median=17 years X^2=1 8064 d.f.=1 .20>P>.10				
Muslims	Younger (up to 17 years)	68	45.95	266	50.89
	Older (above 17 years)	80	54.05	276	49.11
	Total	148		562	
	Median=17 years X^2=0.9863 d.f.=1 50>P>.30				

It is seen that the mean age of Pandits and Muslims is identical at both the places.

The study shows significant results in the case of Pandits in urban areas whereas it is non-significant in the case of Muslims at both the places of study. The conclusions drawn from tables 5.17(a) and (b) would, therefore, be that both Pandits and Muslims have more number of children to women who marry at younger ages. The ratio of fertility in the case of Pandits at Srinagar is 135 : 89 against 110 : 90 of Muslims. The ratio at Sopore for Pandits is 120 : 84 against 111 : 91 of Muslims. Thus there is significant variation in the case of Pandits (Srinagar). The results also support the hyphothesis that younger marriages increase fertility apparently because of longer reproductive period after marriage. It could safely therefore be concluded that a sizeable increase in the age at marriage will definitely reduce the fertility.

IV. Fertility performance and duration of interval between Marriage and '0' Parity

Table 5.18

Fertility Performance and duration of interval between Marriage and '0' Parity among the Kashmiri Pandits and Muslims of Srinagar and Sopore

Population	*Interval between marriage and first child birth*	*No. of women with children (%)*	*No. of live births (%)*
Srinagar			
Pandits	up to 3 years	146 (78.92)	394 (77.10)
	above 3 years	39 (21.08)	117 (22.90)
	$X^2 = 0.2119$ d.f. $= 1$, $.70>P>.50$		
Muslims	up to 3 years	147 (79.46)	550 (77.03)
	above 3 years	38 (20.54)	164 (22.97)
	$X^2 = 0.1541$, d.f. $= 1$, $.70>P>.50$		
Sopore			
Pandits	up to 3 years	85 (69.67)	256 (64.48)
	above 3 years	37 (30.33)	141 (35.52)
	$X^2 = 1.0281$, d.f. $= 1$, $.50>P>.30$		
Muslims	up to 3 years	113 (76.35)	454 (80.78)
	above 3 years	35 (23.65)	108 (19.22)
	$X^2 = 1.0227$, d.f. $= 1$, $.50>P>.30$		

Median = 3 years

The relationship between the interval from marriage to '0' parity and fertility performance has been discussed in Chapter IV. In this chapter we shall study the comparative data in respect of Pandit and Muslim women of Srinagar and Sopore respectively.

It is observed from the table that Muslim (Sopore) mothers with shorter interval between the ages at marriage and '0' Parity have large number of children. In other cases i.e., Pandits (Srinagar and Sopore) and Muslims (Srinagar) women with shorter intervals have lesser number of children. Even so because difference is non-significant (X^2 = 1.0281, 1.0227) no definite relationship between fertility and interval between marriage and '0' Parity can be established.

V. Duration of Married Life and Fertility

An attempt has been made to compare the relation betwəen the duration of married life with fertility in the case of Pandit women (at Srinagar and Sopore) and Muslim women as per table 5.19.

Both, in the case of Pandits and Muslims the difference is significant which proves the hypothesis that the longer the duration of married life, higher is the rate of fertility.

VI. Fertility in relation to level of Literacy

The various aspects of the correlation between literacy and fertility and the various studies carried out in this direction have been examined in the previous chapter. Here an attempt is being made to make a comparative study of the correlation between the two selected populations o: Pandits and Muslims.

Table 5.20 indicates the comparative study of the two populations separately at Srinagar and Sopore.

It will be observed from the table that the average number of live births per marriage decreases with the increase in the level of education in the case of both Pandits and Muslims. The decline is observed maximum when there is a rise in educational level from

Table 5.19

Fertility Performance and Duration of Married Life among the Kashmiri Pandits and Muslims of Srinagar and Sopore

Population	Duration of married life	No. of women No.	No. of women %	No. of live Birth No.	No. of live Birth %
Srinagar					
Pandits	Shorter (up to 18 years)	99	53.51	202	39.53
	Longer (above 18 years)	86	46.49	309	60.47
	Median is 18 years				
	X^2 is 7.5782, d.f. = 1, .01>P>.001				
Muslims	Shorter (up to 16 years)	119	64.32	350	49.02
	Longer	66	35.68	364	50.98
	Median is 16 years				
	X^2 is 7.1281, d.f. = 1, .01>P>.001				
Sopore					
Pandits	Shorter (up to 18 years)	69	56.56	164	41.31
	Longer (above 18 years)	53	43.44	233	58.69
	Median is 18 years				
	X^2 is 6.1335, d.f. = 1, .02>P>.01				
Muslims	Shorter (up to 17 years)	79	53.38	217	38.62
	Longer (above 17 years)	69	46.62	345	61.38
	Median is 17 years				
	X^2 is 7.7813, d.f. = 1, .01>P>.001				

Table 5.20

Fertility vis-a-vis level of literacy among the Kashmiri Pandits and Muslims of Srinagar and Sopore

Educational level	*Pandits*			*Muslims*		
	No. of women	*%*	*Average No. of live births*	*No. of women*	*%*	*Average No. of live births*
Srinagar						
No formal Education	36	19.46	3.83	124	67.02	4.02
Middle School	30	16.22	3.20	28	15.14	2.82
Secondary School	56	30.27	2.55	15	8.11	2.73
Graduate	46	24.86	1.47	3	1.62	2.67
Post-graduate and above	17	9.19	1.44	15	8.11	1.8
Sopore						
No formal education	55	45.08	3.99	115	77.70	3.93
Middle School	14	11.48	2.78	10	6.76	1.43
Secondary School	31	25.41	2.41	15	10.14	1.53
Graduate	19	15.57	1.68	6	4.05	1.8
Post-graduate and above	3	2.46	1.66	2	1.35	1.5

no formal education to Middle School level in the case of Muslim women both at Srinagar and Sopore, and in the case of Pandit women at Sopore. In the case of Pandit women at Srinagar the maximum decline was observed when there is a rise in education level from Secondary School to Graduation. This conclusion would become all the more clear when it is noted that 71.77 Muslim women have had no formal education (67.02% at Srinagar and 77.7% at Sopore) while Pandit women only 29.64% were without formal education (19.64% at Srinagar and 45.08% at Sopore).

It is, therefore, apparent that population growth in the case of Pandits nnd Muslims living in semi-urban areas can be checked by the rapid spread of education within a reasonably forseeable future. As a long term measure and in the case of urban Pandits the level has to be increased to Secondary School and above in order to achieve reduction in growth rate of population.

Sex of the Child and Fertility : Attitudes to children varies from society to society because of their respective customs, beliefs and traditions. An attempt was, therefore, made to study the difference, if any, of the effect of the sex of 1st two children on family size between Kashmiri Pandits and Muslims at urban and semi-urban places. In the case of both these communities the effect was found to be statistically non-significant as would be seen from the table (5.21).

Table 5.21

Sex of the 1st and 2nd child vis-a-vis Family Size among the Kashmiri Pandits and Muslims of Srinagar and Sopore

Population	*Sex*	*No. of women*	*No. of children*	*Family size*
Srinagar				
Pandits	Both male	49	120	2.45
	1st male	47	125	2.66
	1st female	47	117	2.49
	Both female	42	124	2.95
Muslims	Both Male	57	189	3.32
	1st male	52	177	3.40
	1st female	26	95	3.65
	Both female	53	192	3.62
Sopore				
Pandits	Both male	25	82	3.28
	1st male	40	110	2.75
	1st female	31	87	2.81
	Both female	26	91	3.50
Muslims	Both male	41	135	3.29
	1st male	37	103	2.78
	1st female	28	111	3.96
	Both female	42	154	3.67

Pregnancy wastage and Fertility : Abortions are of two types, voluntary or induced and involuntary or spontaneous. The former is adopted as a measure of family planning. A comparative study of Kashmiri Pandits and Muslims has revealed that induced abortion was adopted by Pandits more than Muslims. Taking into account only involuntary abortions an attempt has been made to study its effect on family size in the case of these two communities. The results have been found to be statistically non-significant.

Table 5.22

Pre-Natal death at 1st and 2nd delivery vis-a-vis Family Size among the Kashmiri Pandits and Muslims of Srinagar and Sopore

Population	*Any Pre-natal death at 1st/ 2nd delivery*	*No. of women*	*No. of children*	*Family size*
Srinagar				
Pandits	Yes	6	13	2.17
	No	179	473	2.64
Muslims	Yes	6	15	2.5
	No	179	638	3.56
Sopore				
Pandits	Yes	5	12	2.4
	No	117	358	3.05
Muslims	Yes	4	11	2.75
	No	144	492	3.42

Fertility Performance and Mortality of Children : Infant mortality at the first or second child birth creates a scare and therefore a sense of insecurity among women, and the fertility increases for fear of loss of children. Even thongh with the improvement all round in hygiene and health the child-mortality has considerably declined. An attempt was made to study the effect of child-mortality on fertility among the two communities but no significant results were arrived at.

Table 5.23

Infant Mortality at '0' and 1st parity vis-a-vis family size among the Kashmiri Pandits and Muslims of Srinagar and Sopore

Population	*Infant mortality suffered*	*No. of women*	*No. of children*	*Family size*
Srinagar				
Pandits	Yes	12	24	2.0
	No	173	462	2.67
Muslims	Yes	21	72	3.43
	No	164	581	3.54
Sopore				
Pandits	Yes	7	18	2.57
	No	115	352	3.06
Muslims	Yes	24	76	3.17
	No	124	427	3.44

Even though the difference is not statistically significant, there is a definite trend that mothers who have suffered infant mortality an 'O' and 1st Parity have lesser number of children than those who have not. This is true of both Kashmiri Pandit and Muslim mother.

Growth Rate of Family Sizes among the Kashmiri Pandits and Muslims

After making an assessment of the impact of various bio-social factors on fertility, of the Pandit and Muslim population samples of Srinagar and Sopore, an attempt has been made to find the extent of net increase in family size to see the trend in the growth rate. The results of the comparison of this rate between Pandits and Muslims have been set out in table (5.24).

Table 5.24

Growth Rate vis-a-vis Family Size among the Kashmiri Pandits and Muslims of Srinagar and Sopore

Populations	*No. of children per family in the year*						
	1962		*1967*		*1972*		*1977*
Srinagar							
Pandits	1.50	(.38)	1.88	(.51)	2.39	(.24)	2.63
Muslims	2.07	(.43)	2.50	(.63)	3.13	(.43)	3.56
Sopore							
Pandits	1.29	(.68)	1.97	(.59)	2.56	(.47)	3.03
Muslims	1.81	(.55)	2.36	(.50)	2.86	(.54)	3.40

The table (5.24) and figure (11) reveals that in Srinagar, the Kashmiri Pandits and Muslims seem to have almost similar rates of growth for the first ten years i. e. from 1962 to 1972. Only in the next five years, the growth rate in terms of increase in the family size has been much greater among the Muslims (.43) than in the Pandits (.24).

However, at Sopore it is observed that for the first ten years i. e. from 1962 to 1972, the growth rate has been greater in the Pandits than in Muslims. But for the next five years Muslims overtake the Pandit and show a slightly higher growth rate (.54) than the Pandits (.47).

Thus it may be inferred that in Srinagar, the cumulative effect of various demographic factors including birth control measures being negligible for the first ten years do not seem to have caused much difference in the growth rate of Pandits and Muslims, but, during the next five years it (effect of bio-demographic factors) has been greater in the Pandits than in Muslims.

However, in Sopore, the cumulative impact of various bio-social demographic factors seems to be greater on the growth rate of Muslims than Pandits during the first ten years but reverse is

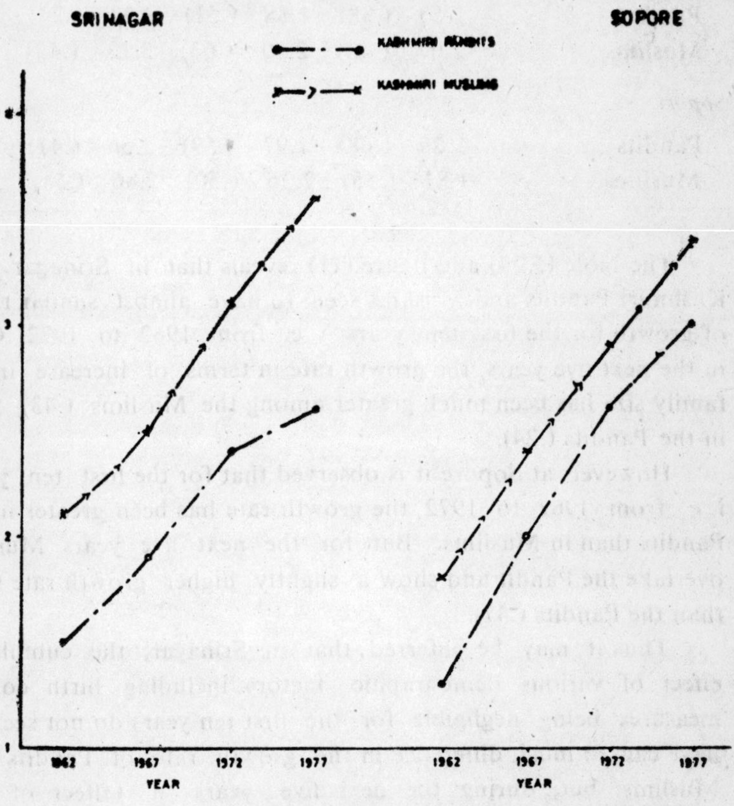

Fig. 11 Growth rate of family size among the Kashmiri Pandits and Muslims

the trend seen in the next five years when this impact seems to be greater in Muslims.

To sum up, it may be said that in view of the results of last five years (1972-1977), the impact of various bio-social demographic factors (which may be responsible for the curbing of further population growth) seems to have been felt more in Pandits than in Muslims, both at Srinagar as well as Sopore.

CHAPTER

6

Fertility in Relation to Body Dimensions

It is a matter of common knowledge that the net increase in the human population is the result of the interplay of the birth and death rates. With the improved economic conditions and better social environment the death rate is decreasing year after year and the life expectancy is increasing. The birth rate and therefore the fertility plays relatively more significant part in population increase. While studying the factors affecting fertility it has become important to study fertility against biological background. After all the state of health and physique of the father and the mother may affect the fecundity. In case a relationship exists between the physical characteristics like height, weight etc., and fertility, it will be possible for us to understand and analyse the effects of these traits (governed by environment as well as by heredity) on human development. Although the stature of a person is mainly determined by genetic influence (Clark, 1956) yet the environmental factors also do affect it to a considerable extent especially the food consumption during various stages of growth (Hsia, 1968). Several studies have been carried out in this field of correlation between fertility and body dimensions. While Eaton and Mayer (1953) studied social biology in relation to fertility. Howells (1953) showed interrelation of birth interval and body size. Clark and Spuhler (1959) also have examined the relation between differential fertility and body dimensions. Their conclusion was that "above average fertility group" had higher body weight than "below average fertility group". No significant difference was found with reference to height. Another study made by Damon and Thomas (1967) showed greater fertility in respect of lean fathers although the study on American Parents conducted by Davenport (1923) showed larger families for stockier parents than slender parents. Height and weight are among the most important morphological variables for finding out the structural, constitutional and psychosomatic background of an individual. The influence of these variables on fertility behaviour is, therefore, an important criteria.

Lasker and Thomas (1976) is of the view that the gradual worldwide increase in stature over the last century is the result of environmental influences and not of any alteration in the pool of genes determining it. But, it is not so in the case of phenotypic selection involving increased fertility with modal anthropometric measurements because it involves normalizing natural selection at the genetic level. Persons of extreme physique like dwarfs and giants have lower fertility. The reason for this according to Laskar and Thomas (1976) is that (in a species where mortality differentials are small) the genetic determinants for extreme physiques are ordinarily selected against through their lower fertility. According to a study conducted in Denmark (Stern, 1960) persons of normal physique had on an average 5 times as many children as had chondrodystrophic dwarfs.

The study conducted by Mitton and Vetta, both in 1975 show that the persons nearer the mean height and in some cases weight have higher than average fertility.

In 1976 Laskar and Thomas carried out a study in Mexico and came to the conclusion that the suggestive evidence included tendencies to decreased variance of limb length measurements in females of high fecundity and greater head length in the reproductively more fit of both the sexes.

In view of the findings of these anthropologists and

demographers, it was thought desirable to carry out a similar study on the Kashmiris.

Anthropometric measurements and relevant demographic informations were taken on 107 unrelated Kashmiri Pandit women and 168 unrelated Kashmiri Muslim women from Srinagar and Sopore, since the two populations from these two places form respectively intermarrying groups, living under quite identical climatic conditions that may influence body growth and/or fertility.

Besides, the urban, semi-urban differences that were observed in the fertility were chiefly the results of socio-economic factors that influence the value system *vis-a-vis* the size of family and a subsequent degree of acceptance of birth control devices. Since the present samples include only those women who (along with their husbands) have never used any birth control device, the factor of urban, semi-urban differences being in fertility, becomes immaterial for these women coming either from Srinagar or from Sopore.

The anthropometric measurements taken according to Martin Seller (Singh and Bhasin, 1968) are : height vertex, body weight, chest girth, hip girth, maximum calf girth, maximum upper arm girth and skinfold at biceps and triceps.

Besides these measurements, Ponderal Index and Muscle and Bone contents were also assessed using the relevant anthropometric measurements.

Age-wise distribution of Kashmiri Pandit and the Muslim women in high and low fertility groups

If there is any one of the chief known influences that one might single out for analysis purposes, it is the age. Data has, therefore, been divided into 5 years cohorts to rate reproductive fitness (No. of births). For each cohort, Mean number of live births has been calculated and accordingly each woman was rated above or below the median for her cohort. Then, the whole data was pooled into 2 groups of high and low fertility—the women having less than mean number of live births for their cohort were grouped into "Low" fertility group and the women having above the mean number of live births were grouped into "High" Fertility group.

Table 6.1

Age-wise distribution of Kashmiri Pandit and the Muslim women in high and low fertility groups

Age-group	*Range for live births*	*Median for live births*	*No. of women in low fertility group*	*No. of women in high fertility group*
Kashmiri Pandits				
15-19	—	—	—	—
20-24	1-2	1.5	2	2
25-29	1-4	1.4	9	18
30-34	1-4	3.2	15	4
35-39	1-4	2.7	9	7
40-44	0-6	3.1	5	1
45 +	0-7	3.5	12	23
Total			52	55
Kashmiri Muslims				
15-19	0-1	0.5	2	2
20-24	0-3	1.5	14	10
25-29	0-5	3.33	26	6
30-34	1-6	3.0	9	16
35-39	1-8	3.4	6	12
40-44	3-8	5.5	7	10
45+	2-8	4.4	16	32
Total			80	88

Table 6.1 gives the age-wise distribution of Kashmiri Pandit and Muslim women in high and low fertility groups respectively. The results from this table have to be viewed in the content of one limitation, that of the possibility of some large influence of cohortson fertility (Lasker and Thomas, 1976). It could be that those born in earlier decades have a reversed trend in relation to

some measure of reproductive fitness of some anthropometric variables from that of later cohorts. Such a relationship would not be apparent from the present anlysis because the cohorts have been pooled.

The two series of high and low fertility have been compared with respect to mean and standard deviation of each anthropometric variable, of Ponderal index and of muscle and bone contents. The variances have been tested by F-test and means have been compared by t-test at 5% level of significance.

Theoretically, 3 types of selection may act on continuous variation in natural populations (Mueller, 1979) :

1. Directional, in which one of the extreme is favoured.
2. Stabilizing, in which the average phenotype is favoured over the extremes; and
3. Disruptive/diversifying, in which extremes have a higher fitness than intermediates.

In the first, fitness has a linear association with a character and in the remaing two, curvilinear association.

In view of these facts, it is expected that the stabilizing (or balancing) selection would show higher variances in the high fertility group for any variable in which it was significantly involved. On the other hand, diversifying selection would also show higher variance in the high fertility group and significant differences in means would point to directional selection.

Height Vertex in Relation to Fertility

Height vertex or stature (as commonly known) is the most crucial measurement which sums up all the linear measurements of the body. This has been regarded as the most common comparable human trait. Several morphological and psychosomatic variables have been examined in relation to stature. Mention may be made of the studies carried out by Davenport (1923), Gini (1934) and Damon (1965). Clark and Sphular (1959), Bailly and Garn (1979), Martorell et al (1981) etc. discussed the relationship between height and fertility.

Table 6.2

Fertility and the Mean Height Vertex of the Kashmiri Pandit and the Muslim women

Population	*Fertility group*	*No. of women*	*Height (cms)* *Mean*	*S.D.*	*S.E.*	*t*	*F*
Pandits							
	Low	52	157.81	6.19	0.86	2.29*	1.145
	High	55	155.12	5.95	0.80		
Muslims							
	Low	80	156.15	6.93	0.78	3.497*	3.559*
	High	88	152.97	4.46	0.48		

*Significant results

Table 6.2 shows the height vertex in relation to high and low fertility groups of Kashmiri Pandits and Muslims respectively.

It is observed that the mean height of women with less children (low fertility group) is higher than those of women with more children (high fertility group) both in Kashmiri Pandits as well as Muslims. Differences between the means in both the populations are statistically significant.

The dispersion also is greater in low fertility group in both the Kashmiri Pandits and the Muslims. For Kashmiri Pandits it is 6.19 as against 5.95 for high fertility group and for Muslims it is 6.93 as against 4.46 for high fertility group. The variance ratio test shows non-significant differences at 5 per cent level in the case of Kashmiri Pandits but the differences is significant in the case of Muslims.

Thus we may say that among the Kashmiri women (both Pandits and Muslims) stature seems to play an important role in determining the fertility and bears a reciprocal relationship with fertility, with the short statured women being more fertile. This is in conformity with the results from some other studies. Clark and Sphuler (1959) found that short individuals tend to be more fertile than tall individuals, the differences being not significant.,

Bailey and Garn (1979) also found high fertility in the short females the differences were found to be significant.

Martorell et al (1961) also observed that shorter women tend to have more number of children than the taller women.

Body Weight and Fertility

The studies conducted in the past do not show any evidence of a dependable relationship between weight of women and their fertility. Damon (1965) has carried out an extensive study in this field. An attempt has been made to evaluate any possible relationship between the weight of women and their fertility in the present study. The mean body weights of the Kashmiri Pandit and Muslim women having high and low fertility respectively have been set in table 6.3.

Table 6.3

Fertility and Mean Body Weight of the Kashmiri Pandit and the Muslim women

Population	*Fertility groups*	*No. of women*	*Weight (kgs)*			*t*	*F*
			Mean	*S.D.*	*S.E.*		
Pandits							
	Low	52	53.94	8.55	1.19	0.518	1.6514*
	High	55	52.94	11.3	1.52		
Muslims							
	Low	80	46.81	6.55	0.74	0.993	1.608*
	High	88	45.63	8.75	0.93		

*Significant results

It is observed that the mean body weight of women in low fertility group is higher than those in the high fertility group in both the populations under study. Though the differences in the means of the body weights were found to be not significant at 5 per cent probability level, but the variance ratio test shows statistically significant value at 5 per cent level in Kashmiri Pandit as well as in

Kashmiri Muslim women indicating that the body weight does play some role in determining the fertility.

Against this Clark and Sphüler (1959) observed that body weight and fertility are positively associated.

Bailey and Garn (1979) also observed that women with higher body weight have higher fertility than the women with lower body weight.

Ponderal Index and Fertility

Body weight along with the height vertex helps in estimating the physique of the individual. Main components of ponderal index being height and weight; it is calculated by dividing the height vertex by the cube root of weight (Singh and Bhasin, 1968). Higher the value of Ponderal Index, the leaner an individual and lower the value of ponderal index, the more stocky an individual would be.

The values of ponderal index in relation to fertility are set out in table 6.4.

It is observed that the average ponderal index among Pandits as well as Muslims is higher for the women of low fertility group than that of the high fertility group. However, the differences were found to be not significant for Pandits as well as Muslims.

Table 6.4

Fertility and Mean Ponderal Index of the Kashmiri Pandit and the Muslim women

Populaiion	*Fertility group*	*No. of women*	*Ponderal Index cm/kg*			*t*	*F*
			Mean	*S. D.*	*S. E.*		
Pandits							
	Low	52	41.98	2.31	0.32	0.406	2.121*
	High	55	41.75	3.46	0.47		
Muslims							
	Low	80	43.51	1.99	0.22	1.271	1.02
	High	88	43 10	2.19	0.23		

*Significant results

The test of variance (F) shows significant differences in case of Pandits but non-significant difference in case of Muslims.

We may, therefore, conclude that though statistically not significant, there is a tendency that the stocky women are more fertile than the lean women among both the Pandits and the Muslims with the Pandits showing significantly higher variability in this respect.

Davenport (1923) drew similar conclusions, that is, stocky parents have higher fertility compared to the lean ones.

Clark and Sphuler (1959) also observed that the stocky parents are more fertile than the lean ones.

Bailey and Garn (1979) also found stocky built to be associated with high fertility among the American women.

The only exceptions are Damon and Thomas (1967) who observed lean fathers having higher fertility than the stocky ones.

Chest Girth in Relation to Fertility

The chest girth is the measurement of the circumference of the chest when breathing normally. While taking the measurement the tape was held horizontally at the level of nipples passing over the lower scapular angle. The arms of the women are slightly raised but not high enough from the horizontal level.

Table 6.5

Fertility and Mean Chest Girth of the Kashmiri Pandit and the Muslim women

Population	*Fertility group*	*No. of woman*	*Chest girth (cms)* Mean	S.D.	S.E.	*t*	*F*
Pandits							
	Low	52	83.31	7.167	0.994	0.661	2.563*
	High	55	88.56	11.80	1.591		
Muslims							
	Low	80	83.87	5.785	0.647	2.538*	1.050
	High	88	81.52	6.218	0.663		

*Significant results

The table (6.5) reveals that the chest girth on an average is greater in the women of high fertility group among the Kashmiri Pandit sample, but the difference is statistically not significant.

However, in the case of Kashmiri Muslim sample, the mean chest girth is greater for the women of low fertility group than that for the women of high fertility group. This difference is found to be significant; we may, therefore, conclude that the women with broader chests tend to be less fertile than the women with smaller chests among the muslims.

However, Tiwari (1974) has found a positive relationship between chest girth and fertility among the Muslim women of East Nimar. Her findings are in conformity with that observed for the present Kashmiri-Pandit sample.

Hip Girth and Fertility

Hip Girth is the measurement of the circumference of the hips at their widest portion.

It is measured with a tape with due care that the woman whose measurement is being taken keeps her feet close to each other. The results of the measurements of hip girth are set out in Table 6.6.

Table 6.6

Fertility and Mean Hip Girth of the Kashmiri Pandit and the Muslim women

Population	*Fertility group*	*No. of women*	*Hip girth (cms)*			*t*	*F*
			Mean	*S.D.*	*S.E.*		
Pandit							
	Low	52	94.72	6.939	0.962	.4261	3.425*
	High	55	95.58	13.207	1.781		
Muslims							
	Low	80	89.07	5.019	0.561	1.003	1.502*
	High	88	88.18	6.452	0.688		

***significant results**

It is observed that the hip girth on an average is greater in the women of high fertility group among the Kashmiri Pandits.

Similar results were obtained by Tiwari (1974) who observed a positive relationship between hip girth and fertility among the Muslims.

The reverse seems to be true in case of Muslims in whom, the mean hip girth is greater in the women of low fertility group.

The differences in both the populations (Pandits as well as Muslims) were found to be non-significant. But the variance ratio (F) was found to be significant in Pandits as well as in Muslims indicating that there is some relationship between hip girth and fertility.

However, with respect to both, the chest girth and the hip girth, the Pandit women with higher fertility show somewhat broader chests and hips than the Muslim women with higher fertility who show somewhat narrower chest and hips compared to the respective women of lower fertility.

Consequently, any generalized trend of relationship between fertility and chest and hip girth is not discernible.

Maximum Calf Girth and Fertility

This is the measurement of the circumference of the calf where calf muscles are most developed. While taking this measurement, the subject was asked to stand with her legs five to 10 cms. apart. The tape was put around the ankle and was slid upwards to bring it at proper position.

It is observed from table (6.7) that the mean calf girth is greater in the low fertility group women among the Kashmiri Pandits. This difference is found to be significant; we may, therefore, say that the Kashmiri Pandit women with lesser calf girth are more fertile.

This is in conformity with the observations made by Tiwari (1974), Bala (1977), Chatterjee and Datta (1981) all of whom have found a negative relationship between calf girth and fertility.

However, among the Kashmiri Muslim women the reverse is

true: among them the mean calf girth is greater in the high fertility group. Though the differences are not significant, the variance ratio test shows significant differences between high and low fertility groups in both Pandit and Muslim women.

Table 6.7

Fertility and Mean Maximum Calf Girth of the Kashmiri Pandits and the Muslim women

Population	*Fertility group*	*No. of women*	*Maximum Calf Girth (cm)* Mean	S.D.	S.E.	*t*	*F*
Pandits							
	Low	52	31.242	2.617	0.363	2.236*	1.619*
	High	55	29.923	3.425	0.462		
Muslims							
	Low	80	29.308	2.501	0.28	.586	13.886*
	High	88	29.941	9.774	1.042		

*significant results

The conclusions drawn in the case of Muslim women are in accordance with those of Clarke and Sphuler (1959) who found a positive relationship between calf girth and fertility in males.

Maximum Upper Arm Girth in Relation to Fertility

The measurement is taken of the maximum circumference of the upper arm horizontally where the biceps muscle are most developed. The girth is measured with a tape at right angles to the axis of the hanging arm. The results of the measurement of Kashmiri Pandit and Muslim women have been set out in table 6.8.

It is observed that the mean maximum upper arm girth is greater in the women of low fertility group in, both, Pandits and Muslims. Further, in case of Pandits the difference was found to be significant.

Table 6.8

Maximum Upper Arm Girth of the Kashmiri Pandit and the Muslim women

Population	Fertility group	No. of women	Max. Upper Arm Girth (cms)			t	F
			Mean	S.D.	S.E.		
Pandits							
	Low	52	25.873	3.344	0.464	2.123*	1.0494
	High	55	24.465	3.516	0.474		
Muslims							
	Low	80	23.852	2.410	0.269	1.703	1.202
	High	88	23.172	2.766	0.295		

*Significant results

Thus we may conclude that women with greater maximum upper arm girth tend to be less fertile than the women with lesser maximum upper arm girth among Kashmiri Pandit and Muslim women. However, Tiwari (1974) found no relationship between upper arm girth and fertility among the muslim women of East Nimar.

Skinfold at Bicep and Fertility

Skinfold measurement provides a means of estimating the amount of fat of the body. It is an indication of the body composition and the calorie aspects of the nutritional status.

The measurement of skinfold at biceps is taken on the anterior side of upper arm by lifting about 1 cm longitudinal fold of the skin with thumb and index finger and making the skinfold measuring caliper exert a uniform pressure of 10 gm/mm.[2]

It is seen from table (6.9) that the mean skinfold at biceps is greater for women in low fertility group among the Kashmiri Pandits while among Muslims it is greater for the women of high fertility group. But with the differences in the mean and dispersion respectively being not significant, we may say that there is no significant association between the fat content at biceps and fertility among Kashmiri Pandit and Muslim women.

Bala (1977) and Chatterjee and Datta (1981) did not find any significant relationship between the fat content at biceps and fertility among the Baniya women of Mehrauli and the Rajput women of Delhi-U.P. Border village respectively.

Table 6.9

Fertility and Mean Skinfold at Biceps of Kashmiri Pandit and the Muslim women

Population	*Fertility group*	*No. of women*	*Skinfold at biceps (mm)*			*t*	*F*
			Mean	*S.D.*	*S.E.*		
Pandits							
	Low	52	8.933	2.88	0.40	1.148	1.056
	High	55	8.275	3.048	0.41		
Muslims							
	Low	80	8.58	2.20	0.246	0.139	1.256
	High	88	8.63	2.59	0.276		

Skinfold at Tricep and Fertility

This measurement indicates the subcutaneous fat at the site of tricep muscle (on the posterior side of the upper arm). The mean of the measurement of skinfold at tricep, their dispersion and variance have been calculated for low fertility group and high fertility group respectively among the Kashmiri Pandit and Muslim women and the results have been set out in Table 6.10.

It is observed that the mean value of skinfold at triceps is greater in the low fertility group women among the Kashmiri Pandits.

The reverse is true in case of Muslims in whom the mean value of skinfolds at triceps is greater in the higher fertility group women.

However, the differences in mean as well as variance ratio are not significant in Pandits as well as in Muslims.

Tablc 6.10

Fertility and Mean Skinfold at Tricep of the Kashmiri Pandit and the Muslim women

Population	*Fertility group*	*No. of women*	*Skinfold at tricep (mm)*			*t*	*F*
			Mean	*S.D*	*S.E*		
Pandits							
	Low	52	15.8	5.20	0.721	1.424	1.165
	High	55	14.4	4.89	0.668		
Muslims							
	Low	80	14.58	3.84	0.430	0.143	1.139
	High	88	14.67	4.31	0.459		

We may, therefore, conclude that no significant trend is observed in case of sub-cutaneous fat at triceps *vis-a-vis* fertility among the Kashmiri women.

Bala (1977) observed that the women with greater subcutaneous fat at tricep are likely to have more children among the Baniyas of Mehrauli.

Bailey and Garn (1979) also found a positive relatiohship between skinfold at tricep and fertility among the American women.

Thus the findings of Bala (1977) and Bailey and Garn (1979) are in accordance with the results obtained in the Kashmiri Muslims women sample in the present study.

But, Chatterjee and Datta (1981) found a negative relationship between skinfold at tricep and fertility among the Rajput women of Delhi-U.P. border, similar to that found among the Kashmiri Pandit women sample of the present study.

Muscle and Bone Content in Women in Relation to Fertility

The muscle and bone content is assessed with the help of maximum circumference of the upper arm and the skin fold at biceps and triceps. The limb is considered as a cylinder. From the circumference (the upper arm girth) which is measured we can calculate the total diameter (d) of the upper arm $C=\pi d$ or $d=C/\pi$). The corrected diameter (D) is calculated by subtracting the thickness of the skinfold plus the subcutaneous layer. This D denotes the amount of musclc and bone. As the skinfold represents two thinckness of the adipose layer, only half of the skinfold is subtracted (Montague, 1960).

Thus $d=C/\pi$

and $D=d-\frac{S_1}{2}-\frac{S_2}{2}$

where C = Maximum girth of the upper arm

d = diameter of the upper arm

D = Muscle and Bone content

S_1 = Skinfold over triceps muscle

S_2 = Skinfold at biceps muscle

The results of muscle and bone content in women in relation to fertility have been set out in table (6.11).

Table 6.11

Fertility and Average Muscle and Bone Content of the Kashmiri Pandit and the Muslim women

Population	*Fertility group*	*No. of women*	*Muscle and Bone Content*			*t*	*F*
			Mean	*S. D.*	*S. E.*		
Pandits	Low	52	6.83	0.89	0.123	1.344	1.296
	High	55	7.08	1.04	0.140		
Muslims	Low	80	6.64	0.98	0.1096	1.837	1.286
	High	88	6.37	0.91	0.097		

It is observed that the muscle and bone content on an average is greater for the women of high fertility group in Kashmiri Pandit sample.

The reverse is true in case of Kashmiri Muslims women in whom lower muscle and bone content is associated with the higher fertility.

The differences in the means in both, Pandits as well as in Muslims are not significant. The respective variances, too, are not significantly different in both the Pandits and Muslims.

We may, therefore, say that there is no significant association between the muscle and bone content on one hand and fertility on the other among the Kashmiri women.

But Chatterjee and Datta (1981) observed, among the Rajput women of Delhi-U.P. border villages, a decrease in fertility with the increase in muscle and bone content.

A short note on Ponderal Index of the Kashmiri Pandits and the Muslim Women and Sex-Ratio of their Children

Several studies have been conducted on the relationship between the physique of fathers, particularly their linearity or stockiness of build and the sex-ratio of their children. Heath (1954) obtained no relationship between the two. Martinez (1956) reported a remarkable relationship between the two. His finding was that lean men had mostly sons and stocky and men of moderate build had more daughters. Damon and Nuttall (1965) have found that stocky men have a higher proportion of sons than lean men. They were, however, not sure of these findings and wanted these to be got independently confirmed. Pernell (1958) concluded that "fathers of linear build however do not appear, by themselvcs, to disturb the usual sex-ratio of children."

The question whether the mothers of linear or stocky build make a contribution towards this seems quite relevant. An attempt has been made to study the association, if any, between the ponderal index of Kashmiri Pandit and Muslim women, respectively, and the sex-ratio of their children.

From table (6.12) and figure (12), it is observed that in the case of Kashmiri Muslims generally the stockier women have lower percentage of sons than the lean mothers with the exception of <38.4 group, where the number of mothers is only two. This confirms the findings of Martinez (1956) who has drawn the same conclusion with reference to the ponderal index of fathers.

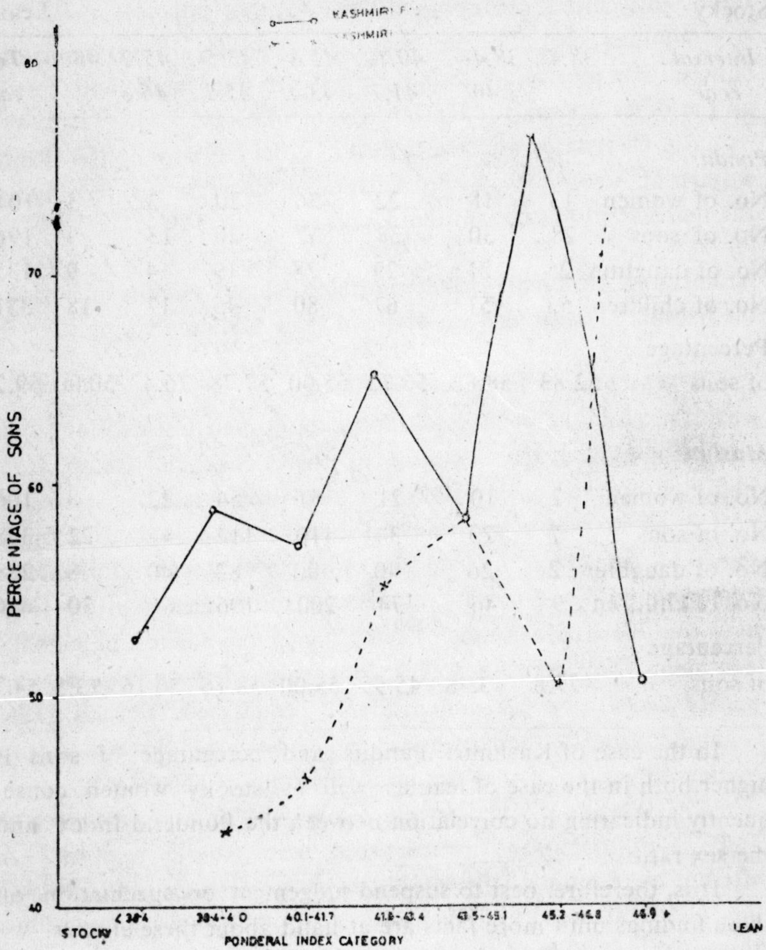

Fig. 12 Percent male children by Ponderal index category for Kashmiri Pandit and Muslim women

Table 6.12

Sex-Ratio of Children of the Kashmiri Pandit and the Muslim women by Ponderal Index Category

Stocky								Lean
Interval code	*<38.4*	*38.4-40*	*40.1-41.7*	*41.8-43.4*	*43.5-45.1*	*45.2-46.8*	*46.9+*	*Total*
Pandits								
No. of women	13	18	22	36	20	3	5	104
No. of sons	28	30	38	52	26	13	9	196
No. of daughter	25	21	29	28	19	4	9	135
No. of children	53	51	67	80	45	17	18	331
Percentage of sons	52.83	58.82	56.72	65.00	57.78	76.47	50.00	59.21
Muslims								
No. of women	2	10	21	51	54	22	8	106
No. of sons	7	20	34	110	114	41	22	348
No. of daughter	2	26	40	90	82	40	8	288
No. of children	9	46	74	200	196	81	30	636
Percentage of sons	77.8	43.48	45.95	55.00	58.16	50.16	73.3	54.72

In the case of Kashmiri Pandits and percentage of sons is higher both in the case of lean as well as stocky women consequently indicating no correlation between the Ponderal Index and the sex ratio.

It is, therefore, best to suspend judgement or speculation on these findings until more facts are at hand about these studies.

CHAPTER

7

Inter-Population Comparison of Body Dimensions vis-a-vis Fertility Level

EVOLUTION, according to Laskar and Thomas (1976), is caused by differences in the number of offsprings left by individuals of different genotypes. The number of offsprings left, is, of course, fully accounted for by two demographic variables : Fertility and Motality. In recent decades human mortality rates of all age groups prior to the end of the reproductive period have dropped sharply. Thereafter the relative significance of fertility differentials for human evolution have increased.

An attempt was, therefore, made in the previous chapter to understand the sort of correlation that may exist between fertility and body dimensions of the Kasnmiri Pandit and the the Kashmiri Muslim women.

In this Chapter, an attempt has been made to make an inter-population comparison of Kashmiri Pandits and Muslims with respect of their body dimensions in low and high fertility groups respectively. The idea is to assess whether the Kashmiri Pandits and Muslims differ with respect of their body dimensions in a particular fertility group.

For this purpose, some representative measurements have been taken — Height as a dimensional variable, Weight and Ponderal index as a density indicator, Girths at chest, hip, calf and upper arm to give an indication of general body build, skinfolds at bicep and tricep as a direct measure of fat and the muscle and bone content.

All these measurements in high and low fertility groups, respectively, have been compared between the Kashmiri Pandit and Kashmiri Muslim women.

Height Vertex of Kashmiri Pandit and Muslim Women

Table 7.1

Mean Height Vertex (S.D. and S.E.) among the Low and High Fertility group of Kashmiri Pandit and Muslim women

Fertility Group	*Population*	*No. of women*	*Height Vertex (cm)*			*t*	*F*
			Mean	*S.D*	*S.E.*		
Low							
	Pandits	52	157.81	6.19	0.86	1.42	1.216
	Muslims	80	156.15	6.93	0.78		
High							
	Pandits	55	155.12	5.95	0.80	2.305*	2.777*
	Muslims	88	152.97	4.46	0.48		

*Significant results

From table (7.1), it is observed that in both the lower and higher fertility groups, the Kashmiri Pandit women are taller than the Muslim women, though the differences are significant in high fertility group of women only.

Body Weight of Kashmiri Pandit and Muslim women.

Table 7.2 reveals that the Body weight of Pandit women is significantly greater than that of Muslim women in both the low fertility and the high fertility groups, respectively.

Table 7.2

Mean Body Weight (S.D. and S.E.) among the Low and High Fertility group of Kashmiri Pandit and Muslim women

Fertility Group	*Population*	*No. of women*	*Body Weight (kgs) Mean*	*S.D.*	*S.E.*	*t*	*F*
Low							
	Pandits	52	53.94	8.55	1.19	5.088*	2.586*
	Muslims	80	46.81	6.58	0.74		
High							
	Pandits	55	52.94	11.3	1.52	4.255*	2.671*
	Muslims	88	45.63	8.75	0 93		

*Significant results

Ponderal Index of Kashmiri Pandit and Muslim women

From table (7.3), it is observed that the ponderal index of the Kashmiri Pandit women is significantly lower than that of Kashmiri Muslims women in both low fertility group as well as in high fertility group.

Therefore, it may be inferred that the Kashmiri Pandit women in both the reproductive categories are significantly more robust than the respective muslim women.

Table 7.3

Mean Ponderal Index (S.D. and S.E) among the Low and High Fertility group of Kashmiri Pandit and Muslim women.

Fertility Group	*Population*	*No.of women*	*Ponderal Index (cm/kg) Mean*	*S.D.*	*S.E.*	*t*	*F*
Low							
	Pandits	52	41.98	2.31	0.32	3.940*	2.116*
	Muslims	80	43.51	1.99	0.22		
High							
	Pandits	55	41.75	3.46	0.47	2.581*	4.176*
	Muslims	88	43.1	2.19	0.23		

*Significant results

Chest Girth of Kashmiri Pandit and Muslim women

Table (7.4) reveals that the chest girth of Pandit women in both the high fertility and low fertility groups is found to be on an overage significantly greater than that of respective Muslim women.

Table 7.4

Mean Chest Girth (S D. and S.E.) of Low and High Fertility group of Kashmiri Pandit and Muslims women

Fertility Group	*Population*	*No. of women*	*Chest Girth (cms)* *Mean*	*S.D.*	*S.E.*	*t*	*F*
Low							
	Pandits	52	87.31	7.167	0.994	2.9005*	2.360*
	Muslims	80	83.87	5.785	0.647		
High							
	Pandits	55	88.56	11.80	1.591	4.084*	5.758*
	Muslims	88	81.52	6.218	0.663		

*Significant results

Hip Girth of Kashmiri Pandit and Muslim women

From table (7.5) it is observed that the hip girth of Pandit women in both the high fertility and low fertility groups is found to be on an average significantly greater than that of respective Muslim women.

Table 7.5

Mean Hip Girth (S.D. and S.E.) among the Low and High Fertility group of Kashmiri Pandit and Muslim women

Fertility Group	*Population*	*No. of women*	*Hip Girth (cms)* *Mean*	*S.D.*	*S.E.*	*t*	*F*
Low							
	Pandits	52	94.72	6.939	0.962	5.074*	2.941*
	Muslims	80	89.07	5.019	0.561		
High							
	Pandits	55	95.58	13.207	1.781	3.876*	6.701*
	Muslims	88	88.18	6.452	0.688		

*Significant results

Maximum Calf Girth of Kashmiri Pandit and Muslim women

With respect to calf girth, as seen from table (7.6), the Kashmiri Pandit women of low fertility group are found to have significantly greater girth than the respective Kashmiri Muslim women.

Table 7.6

Mean Maximum Girth (S.D. and S.E.) among the Low and High Fertility groups of Kashmiri Pandit and Muslim women.

Fertility Group	*Population*	*No. of women*	*Max. Calf girth (cms)*			*t*	*F*
			Mean	*S.D.*	*S.E*		
Low							
	Pandits	52	31.242	2.617	0.363	0.223*	1.681
	Muslims	80	29.308	2.501	0.28		
High							
	Pandits	55	29.923	3 425	0.462	0.0158	5 087*
	Muslims	88	29.941	9.774	1.042		

*Significant results

But, in the high fertility group, it is the Muslim women who have a somewhat greater calf girth than their respective Pandit women though the difference between them is not significant.

Maximum Upper Arm Girth of Kashmiri Pandit and Muslim women

It is observed from table (7.7) that the maximum upper arm girth of Kashmiri Pandit women is significantly greater than that of Muslim women in, both, the low fertility and the high fertility groups, respectively.

Table 7.7

Mean Maximum Upper Arm Girth (S.D. and S.E.) among the Low aud High Fertility group of Kashmiri Pandit and Muslim women.

Fertility group	Population	No. of women	Max. Upper Arm Girth (cm) Mean	S.D.	S.E.	t	F
Low							
	Pandits	52	25.873	3.344	0.464	3.770*	2.975*
	Muslims	80	23.852	2.410	0.269		
High							
	Pandits	55	24 465	3.516	0.474	2.317*	2.582*
	Muslims	88	23.172	2.766	0.295		

*Significant results

Skinfold at Bicep of Kashmiri Pandits and Muslim Women

Table 7.8

Mean Skinfold at Bicep (S.D. and S.E.) among the Low and High Fertility group of Kashmiri Pandit and Muslim women

Fertility group	Population	No. of women	Skinfold at bicep (mm) Mean	S D.	S.E.	t	F
Low							
	Pandits	52	8.933	2.88	0.40	0.752	2.644*
	Muslims	80	8.58	2.20	0.246		
High							
	Pandits	55	8.275	3.048	0.41	0.729	2.144*
	Muslims	88	8.63	2.59	0.276		

*Significant results

With respect to skinfold at biceps, as seen from table 7.8, the Kashmiri Pandit women of low fertility group have slightly larger skinfold at biceps than the respective Kashmiri Muslim women though the difference between them is not significant.

But in the high fertility group, it is the Muslim womem who have a somewhat larger skinfold at bicep than their respective Pandit women though the difference between them also is not significant.

Skinfold at Tricep of Kashmiri Pandit and Muslim women

Table (7.9) reveals that with respect to skinfold at triceps, the Kashmiri Pandit women of low fertility group have slightly larger skinfold at triceps than the respective Kashmiri Muslim women though the difference between them is not significant.

But in the high fertility group, it is the Muslim women who have a somewhat larger skinfold at triceps than their respective Pandit women though the difference between them also is not significant.

Table 7.9

Mean Skinfold at Tricep (S.D. and S.E.) among the Low and High Fertility group of Kashmiri Pandit and Muslim women

Fertility group	*Population*	*No. of women*	*Skinfold at tricep (mm)*			*t*	*F*
			Mean	*S.D.*	*S.E.*		
Low							
	Pandits	52	15.8	5.20	0.721	1.452	2.798*
	Muslims	80	14.58	3.84	0.431		
High							
	Pandits	55	14.4	4.89	0.668	0.333	2.118*
	Muslims	88	14.67	4.31	0 459		

*Significant results

Muscle and Bone Content of Kashmiri Pandits and Muslim women

Table (7.10) reveals that in both the low and the high fertility groups, the Kashmiri Pandit women have greater muscle and bone content than the Muslim women, though the differences are significant in high fertility group of women only.

It may, therefore, be inferred that the Kashmiri Pandit women and the Kashmiri Muslim women belonging to the low fertility group respectively differ significantly with respect to body weight, ponderal index, chest and hip girth, maximum calf and upper arm girth, with Kashmiri Pandit women being heavier, more robust and of broader chests, wider hips and larger maximum calf and upper arm girths than the Muslim women.

Table 7.10

Mean Muscle and Bone Content (S.D. and S.E.) among the Low and High Fertility group of Kashmiri Pandit and Muslim women

Fertility Group	Population	No. of women	Muscle and Bone Content Mean	S.D.	S.E.	t	F
Low							
	Pandits	52	6.83	0.89	0.123	1.1515	1.259
	Muslims	80	6.64	0,98	0.1096		
High							
	Pandits	55	7.08	1.04	0.140	4.176*	2.083*
	Muslims	88	6.37	0.71	0.097		

*Significant results

In the high fertility group, the Kashmiri Pandit women and the Kashmiri Muslim women differ significantly with respect to height, body weight, ponderal index, chest and hip girths, maximum upper arm girth and muscle and bone contents, with the Kashmiri Pandit women being taller, heavier, more robust with broader chests, wider hips, larger maximum upper arm girth and greater muscle and bone content than the Muslim women.

The variance ratio test (F) indicates significant differences between the low fertility group Pandit women and the low fertility group Muslim women in the distribution of body weight, ponderal index, chest and hip girths, upper arm girth and skinfold at biceps and triceps.

However, no significant differences have been observed for the distribution of height vertex, maximum calf girth and muscle and bone content.

Further, the variance ratio test (F) indicates significant differences between the high fertility group Pandit women and the high fertility group Muslim women in the distribution of height vertex, body weight, ponderal index, chest and hip girths, maximum calf and upper arm girths, skinfold at biceps and triceps and the muscle and bone contents.

Thus, these observed differences between the Kashmiri Pandit women and the Kashmiri Muslim women with respect to their body dimensions in the high and low fertility levels may be partly due to genetic differences between the two populations and partly due to better nourishment of the Kashmiri Pandit women, while living under the similar geographical environment.

Till a few centuries ago, the now Kashmiri Muslims and Pandits had shared a common gene pool to a large extent but because of political and historical reasons, most of the Pandits embraced Islam and were therefore matrimonially disconnected with those who remained as Pandits.

It is suprising that in such a short period of time, the women of two populations have come to differ with so many physical characteristics that may have a bearing on fertility. One of the factors that may be responsible for this fast speed of differentiation may be the considerable differences in the marriage pattern of the two populations with muslim population preferring marriage between the near blood relatives and the Pandits desisting from it.

CHAPTER

8

Summary and Conclusion

PROBLEM

ONE OF THE several ways the name Kashmir has been explained is that it is a compound of three sanskrit words : Ka (water), ashm (Rock or mountain) and ir (drain out). In other words Kashmir is that land whose water was drained out through mountains to make it inhabitable. This according to Neelamatpurana was done by Kashyap sage. Soon the land was inhabited by upper caste Brahmins and lower caste Nisadas, Kiratas, Dombas and Chandalas etc. In due course of time people belonging to different ethnic groups and different races migrated to Kashmir and maPe it their permanent home. These included Sakas, Kusans, Huns, Gujars and Tibetans. The population that emerged in this valley finally was that of Kashmiri Pandits who are considered to be purest descendants of the Indo-Aryan race. Kashmir was thus not only inhabited by these Hindus (called Pandits) but was also ruled by Hindu kings belonging to various dynasties up to the end of 13th century. For brief period towards the end, the reign passed into the hands of a Buddhist ruler Ranchan (known by Kashmiris as Renchan Shah) who under the influence of a saint Bulbulshah embraced Islam. But the rule on his death passed again into the hands of his Hindu queen Kota Rani. The Muslim rule came to the valley in 1339 when Shah Mir usurped the throne from her. With this started the conversion of Hindus into Islam forced by the rulers like Sikandar and aided by the Sayyads of of Hamadan. With the passage of time the valley became a Muslim majority area.

Thus the two population groups, the Kashmiri Pandits and the Kashmiri Muslims though at one time constituted ethnically one homogeneous population came to differ from each other in faith and customs and had snapped the marital ties with each other.

After 1947 when India attained independence a large section of Kashmiri Pandits migrated from Kashmir (at higher altitude) to low altitude plains, particularly to Delhi.

It was with this background that the present study was undertaken with a view to investigate as to what extent change in socio-religio-economic status, and the physical environment has so far been able to diversify the bio-demographic patterns of the Kashmiri population. While on the one hand comparison has been made between these two religion based communities Muslims and Pandits, on the other, Urban and semi-urban Pandits and Muslims constituting two major socio-economic groups have also been compared. So far it were the rural urban differentiation in bio-demographic patterns that have been much emphasized. But, in the present study, the comparison between the urban the semi-urban populations in India have started swelling in number much faster at the cost of the rural population and these semi-urban populations therefore require special attention from bio-demographic point of view. The data relating to Pandits of Delhi has provided an insight into the effects of changed environment (including change in altitude) and character of urban cosmopolitan atmosphere.

Further, an assessment has been made of the association that may exist between fertility and body dimensions among the Pandits and Muslims of Kashmir to reveal the differentiation, if any, in this respect too.

Methods and Materials

For the collection of data, an open ended questionnaire was used together with the interview method. To avoid any bias, the households were selected at random from various localities in Srinagar, Sopore and Delhi to give a representative population of these areas. While no selection or distinction as such was made while collecting the sample, the closely related married women were avoided as far as possible. For this purpose, only one married women was taken from each household. These women from each household acted as our primary informants.

For the detailed study of variations in fertility and mortality behaviour and use of birth control devices, the sample consists of 406 Kashmiri Pandit women (Srinagar 185, and Sopore 122 and Delhi 99) and 333 Kashmiri Muslim women (Srinagar 185 and Sopore 148). Data regarding fertility and physique has been taken on 107 Kashmiri Pandit women and 168 Kashmiri Muslim women from Srinagar and Sopore.

Results

After collecting the data from the door to door survey, the data was analysed and the following important features emerged thereby.

Sex Composition

It is observed that in general the Kashmiri population is masculine in character (because of a preponderance of males over females) irrespective of whether they are Hindus or Muslims by faith and irrespective of whether they belong to urban or semi-urban areas. The sex-ratio in all these population samples under study being less than 1000 is similar to that found in the total Indian population and in the J & K state as a whole (1971 census).

However, while the Pandits of Srinagar and Sopore and Muslims of Srinagar reveal a lower proportion of females in the child bearing age than in the pre-child bearing age, the Pandits of Delhi and Muslims of Sopore show an increase in the proportion of females in the reproductive age group from the preceeding pre-child bearing age group, which is bound to influence the relative population growth of the populations under consideration with the Pandits of Delhi and the Muslims of Sopore being at a greater risk of population growth; but whether this materialises or not would depend upon a number of other important factors like the socio-economic conditions and the degree of use of birth control measures.

In the post-child bearing age, the proportion of females is further reduced in all the population samples of Kashmiri Pandits and Muslims, which indicate a higher post-reproductive female mortality in both the Pandits and the Muslims.

Age Composition

The age-distributions of the urban and semi-urban Kashmiri Pandits and Muslims reveals that the population size has started shrinking for the last 20 years among the Kashmiri Pandits of Delhi (20-24 years of age group having maximum population percentage), while among the rest of the Kashmiri Pandit and Muslim population belonging to both Srinagar and Sopore respectively, the population size has started shrinking only for the last ten years (maximum population percentage being in the 5-9 years age group).

Further, in the 0-4 year's age group, the Kashmiri Pandits of Delhi have the lowest population percentage while the highest percentage is found among the Muslims of Sopore. This indicates that the maximum impact of various socio-economic factors, including that of family planning, on fertility has been highest among the Kashmiri Pandits of Delhi and least among the Muslims of Sopore. Rest of the population sample under study hold the intermediary positions.

When the concept of "young", "mature" and "old" populations is applied to the population samples under consideration, it is seen that the Kashmiri Pandits and Muslims of Srinagar and Sopore are "young" populations having lower life expectancy than the Kashmiri Pandits of Delhi who can be termed as "mature".

Also, the Kashmiri Pandits and Muslims of Srinagar and Sopore respectively, have an almost 10 year lower median age than the Kashmiri Pandits of Delhi. This again indicates a much higher life expectancy of Delhi Pandits compared to any other population under study, which may be directly the result of better socio-economic and medical conditions prevailing for the Kashmiri Pandit of Delhi than for the presently studied other populations.

From the dependency ratio as well, there is a clear indication of Delhi Pandits being much better off than the Kashmiri Pandits of Srinagar and Sopore respectively. But the Kashmiri Pandits of Srinagar and Sopore seem to be only marginally economically better than the Kashmiri Muslims of the respective areas.

Marriage-wise Distribution

From the percentage frequency of consanguineous marriages, it appears that the risk of having malformed children and of infant mortality should be greatest among the muslims of Sopore, followed by the muslims of Srinagar and least among the Pandit populations. Since the Muslim populations of Kashmir is only about thirty generations old, the selection-relaxation *vis-a-vis* incompatibility effects may not be of significant consequence.

Birth Control

'3' being the desired number of children of all the Kashmiri populations, under consideration, the national slogan appears to have made its desired impact on the Kashmiri populations. However, it is realised profitably only among the Kashmiri Pandits of Srinagar (only among the users of birth control devices) while among the other populations under study, it is yet to be realised.

Relatively speaking the impact of birth control devices as measured in the terms of the difference between the desired and the observed number of children (voluntary effect) seems to be attained the most among the Kashmiri Pandits of Srinagar and the least among the Kashmiri Pandits of Delhi, while the Kashmiri Muslims of Srinagar, Kashmiri Pandits of Sopore and the Kashmiri Muslims of Sopore occupy the intermediary positions in this respect.

The involuntary effect, as judged from the values for the differences in the desired and the observed number, for non-users of birth control devices is totally lacking among the Kashmiri populations irrespective of religion and socio-economic, cultural and or environmental differences.

Among all the Kashmiri populations under consideration, the desired average number of sons is much higher than the desired average number of daughters in both the categories of parents (users and non-users of b.c.d.*). Though among the b.c.d. non-users, this desire is fulfilled among all the five populations, among the b.c.d. users, this desire seems to be fulfilled only among the Pandits of Kashmir.

This (observed ratio of sons to daughters) may be one of the factors responsible for a lower than the desired mean number of children among the b.c.d. users of the Kashmiri Pandits of Srinagar and for the non-achievement of the desired impact of birth control practice among the b.c.d. users of the remaining four populations. The fulfilment of the desired ratio of the sex of the children among the b.c.d. non-users may directly be a function of large average number of children realised than among the b.c.d. users in whom the fertility is deliberately inhibited.

The overall picture that emerged from the frequency of users (48%) and non-users (52%) of birth control devices is not very encouraging and much is needed to be done to bring more and more families into the fold of family planning programme among the Kashmiri Pandits and Muslims.

From the age-wise distribution of users and non-users of birth control measures, it is seen that the maximum percentage of b.c.d. users is among the couples in whom the b.c.d. users age ranges from 15-29 years among the Pandits and in the above 45 years of age-group among the Muslims; 15-29 years age group being the optimum fertility period (as shown by the age-specific fertility rates), it seems that the maximum threat of population explosion is from Kashmiri Muslims (especially Muslims of Sopore) than from the Pandits.

Also, among the Kashmiri Muslims more reliable methods

*b. c. d. =birth control device.

like sterilization and condoms are favoured less than among the Kashmiri Pandits.

Another significant point to be observed is that as high as 87 per cent of Kashmiri Muslim couples and 73 per cent of Kashmiri Pandit couples of Sopore are non-users of birth control devices whatsoever, and pose a much greater threat of population explosion compared to their urban counterparts—in whom the frequency of non-users being about 53 per cent among the Muslims and 19 to 28 per cent amont the Pandits. Among the urban samples it is the Muslims who pose more than 90 per cent risk of population explosion on this score than thc Kashmiri Pandits.

In any case the risk of population explosion on account of non-use of birth control devices is greater for the Muslim population, than for the respective Pandit populations. It is found to be as high as at least 90 per cent for the urban muslims and about 19 per cent for the semi-urban Muslims. For a successful family planning drive among these populations, these relative frequencies of users and non-users of birth control devices have to be borne in mind.

From the point of view of effect of economic status on the use of birth control devices, no particular trend is observed between the various income levels and the use of birth control devices with respect to the population under consideration.

However, from the point of view of type of family, it is seen that there is a higher percentage frequency of "users" than of "non-users" among the women of nuclear families rather than of joint families. Maximum risk of population growth is therefore from the muslims of Sopore (having least percentage frequency of nuclear families) and least from the Pandits of Delhi (having maximum percentage frequency of nuclear families).

Also, with the increase in the level of education of women, more and more women can be brought into the fold of birth control programme and reduce the birth rate to the desired levels, though much more education would be needed for Muslim women than for the Kashmiri Pandit women.

Intra-Population variation with respect of fertility and mortality

(*a*) *Urban Pandits versus Semi-Urban Pandits :* Among the Pandit populations while comparing the urban sample from Srinagar and semi-urban sample from Sopore with respect to their fertility, it is observed that the latter has much higher child-woman ratio, crude birth rate, general fertility rate and total Fertility Rate respectively than the former.

In fact child-woman ratio of semi-urban Pandits is twice than that of the urban Pandits. Total Fertility Rate indicates that while the parents in the urban Pandits sample are just about replacing themselves, in the semi-urban Pandit sample, they are nearly doubling themselves. Thus while the urban Pandit population of Srinagar is eventually likely to become almost stable, the semi-urban Pandit population seems to be still growing in size. The lower natality of urban Pandits of Srinagar *vis-a-vis* the semi-urban Pandits may be partly explained due to the former using the birth control devices about three times (72% of the couples using birth control devices) than that of the latter (only 27% of the couples using the birth control devices).

It has been observed that the maximum decrease in the number of live births per marriage is from the non-formally educated women to middle school level women among all these populations. In view of this, the lower natality of the urban Kashmiri Pandit women may be also because the number of women among them with formal education is nearly one and a half times greater (80%) than those of semi-urban Pandit women (55%).

The average number of conceptions, child birth index and survival index are higher among the semi-urban Pandits than among the urban Pandits indicating higher fertility among the former than the latter.

Also, the percentage frequency of Pre-natal and Post-natal death respectively is much higher among the urban than among the semi-urban Pandits.

It is observed that the mean interval between two parities is longer among the urban Pandits of Srinagar (3.29 years) than among the semi-urban Pandits (2.93 years). As a result of this, the risk of having malformed children associated with the advancing maternal age (35 years onwards) is earlier (in terms of parity) among the urban Pandits of Srinagar than in the semi-urban Pandits of Sopore as the threshold of 34 years is crossed after the fourth parity in the former while in the latter it is crossed after the fifth parity.

However, there is a higher percentage of children born, to mothers above 35 years of age among the semi-urban Pandits than among the urban, and therefore greater chances of children with malformities, associated with the advancing maternal age, are among the former than the latter.

No significant differences were observed between urban and semi-urban Pandits with respect to the length of reproductive period as assessed from the age at menarche and the age at menopause.

The urban-semi-urban factor does not hold true while studying its effects on age at marriage of women, length of interval between marriage and the '0' parity, duration of married life, sex of the first two children, pre-natal deaths occured at first and/or second conception and post-natal deaths (below 1 year of age) occurred at first and/or second conception, respectively upon the fertility performance of women.

(*b*) *Migrant Pandits of Delhi versus Pandits of Kashmir*

However, while comparing the migrant urban Kashmiri Pandit population sample (of Delhi) with the urban Pandits of Srinagar and semi-urban Pandits of Sopore respectively, with respect to their fertility, it is observed that the migrant urban Pandits of Delhi have much higher crude birth rate and total fertility rate than the urban and the semi-urban Pandits respectively of Kashmir.

The crude birth rate of the migrant Pandits of Delhi is twice that of the urban Pandits of Srinagar and is slightly higher than that of the semi-urban Pandits of Sopore also. From the total fertility rate, it appears that while the parents in the urban Pandit sample from Srinagar are just about replacing themselves and in the semi-urban Pandit sample, they are nearly doubling themselves, among the migrant Pandits of Delhi, they are nearly trebling themselves. Thus the situation in case of Pandits of Delhi seems to be rather alarming from the point of view of population growth, considering the fact that 80% of the couple among the migrant Pandits of Delhi are users of birth control devices and nearly 76% of the women are formally educated. It is quite probable that the average duration of the married life which is much larger among the migrant Pandits (25 years) than the urban and semi-urban Pandits (18 years) of Kashmir may be partly the cause of higher fertility among the former than the latter. The differences of natality between Pandits of Kashmir and Delhi may also be partly the effect of attitude on fertility (Clegg and Harrison, 1971) with the Kashmiri Pandits of Kashmir, though using birth control devices to much lesser extent than the Kashmiri Pandits of Delhi, having lower natality than the Kashmiri Pandits of Delhi. Differences in the length reproductive period as assessed from the menarcheal age and menopausal age may be partly responsible for the differences in the natality of the migrant Pandits of Delhi and the Pandits of Kashmir, with the former having longer reproductive span (36.1 years) than the latter (About 33 years).

The migrant Pandits of Delhi differ from the Pandit populations of the valley with respect to their pattern of age-specific fertility rates also—while the urban and semi-urban Pandits of Kashmir have their peak-fertility period from the age of 20 to 24 years, the migrant urban Pandits of Delhi have their peak fertility period from 25 to 29 years of age.

However, from the gross production rate, it appears that all three Pandit population samples share in common the threat of severe deficiency of females in the reproductive age group, which in future may lead to shrinking of these populations. Genetically, there is likely to be a reduction in the frequency of X-linked lethal genes in all the three Pandit populations under consideration.

The migrant Pandits of Delhi have a higher average number of conception than the Pandits of Kashmir. Their (Delhi Pandits) child birth index and survival index is higher than the respective index of semi-urban Pandits of Sopore. Greater reproductive fitness of the migrant Pandits of Delhi *vis-a-vis* Pandits of Kashmir is also exhibited by the much lower percentage frequency of pre-natal deaths among the former than among the latter.

It is observed that the mean interval between two parties is shorter among the migrant Pandits of Delhi (about 2 years) than among the Pandits of Kashmir (around 3 years). As a result of this, the risk of having malformed children associated with the advancing maternal age (35 years onwards) is not found among the former (threshold of 34 years of age is not crossed at all) while among the latter, likelihood of risk of having such children is involved after the fourth-fifth parity when the threshold of 34 years of age is crossed.

In fact, in terms of quantity as well, there is a much lower percentage of frequency of children born to mothers of above 35 years of age and below 20 years of age, respectively among the migrant Pandits of Delhi than among the Pandits of Kashmir, indicating thereby lesser possibility of genetically abnormal children being produced among the former than among the latter.

However, the migrant Pandits of Delhi resemble the Pandits of Kashmir with respect to the effect of age at marriage of women, length of interval between marriage and the '0' parity, sex of the first two children, pre-natal deaths occurred at first and/or second conception and post-natal deaths (below 1 year of age) occurred at first and/or second conception, respectively upon the fertility performance of women.

(*c*) *Urban Muslims versus Semi-Urban Muslims*

Among the Kashmiri Muslim populations, while comparing the urban sample from Srinagar and semi-urban sample from Sopore with respect to their fertility, it is observed that the latter has much higher child-woman ratio, crude birth rate, general fertility rate, total fertility rate and gross reproduction rate respectively than the former. The child-woman ratio and the crude birth rate among the semi-urban Muslims is more than one and a half times greater than those among the urban Muslims. General fertility rate of semi-urban Muslims is almost twice that of urban Muslims. From the total fertility rate, it appears that while in the urban sample, the parents are replacing them three times, in the semi-urban sample, they are replacing them four times. The gross reproduction rate indicates that among the urban Muslims, only two girls are born to every women of child-bearing age while four girls are born to every woman of child bearing age among the semi-urban Muslims. Thus the threat of future population growth among the semi-urban Mnslims is twice that of urban Muslims and the possibility of increased recessive X-linked lethal genes in the same proporation. The lower fertility of urban Muslims of Srinagar *vis-a-vis* the semi-urban Muslims of Sopore may be partly because of the former using the birth control devices about four times (of the couples using birth control devices) than that of the latter (in whom only 13 per cent of the couples are using the birth control devices). Another reason for the lower fertility among urban Muslims may be because there is about 10 per cent higher percentage frequency of women with formal education than among the semi-urban Muslims. Longer reproductive span (as measured from the menarcheal and menopausal ages) of semi-urban Muslim females (36.1 years) than that of the urban Muslim females (33.3 years) may be another reason of higher fertility among the former than the latter.

Though the average number of conceptions of urban and semi-urban Muslim samples is similar, the child birth index and survival index is higher and percentage frequency of pre-natal and post-natal deaths are lower among the former than among the latter.

It is observed that the mean interval between two parties being similar among the urban and semi-urban Muslims (about 2 years), the risk of malformed children being produced associated with the advancing maternal age (women of above 34 years age) (parity-wise) is after the sixth parity in both the populations.

reason for higher fertility among the Muslims than among the Pandits at these places.

The average number of conceptions, child birth index and survival index respectively are higher in Kashmiri Muslims than in Pandits at Srinagar and Sopore respectively; this again indicates higher fertility among the former than the latter.

The percentage frequency of pre-natal and post-natal deaths is, however, higher among the Muslims than among the Pandits of Srinagar and Sopore respectively, indicating higher genetic load among the Muslims than among the Pandits of these areas.

Parity-wise, the threshold of 34 years is crossed by Pandit women much earlier (after fourth and fifth parity) than among the Muslim women (after sixth parity) of Srinagar and Sopore respectively. This is so, because of the fact that on an average, the mean interval between two parities is three years among the Pandits and only two years among the Muslims of Srinagar and Sopore, respectively.

It seems, therefore the risk of having genetically malformed children is much earlier (with regard to parity) among the Pandits than among the Muslims of these places.

Qnantity-wise, however, while at Srinagar the percentage frequency of children produced to women of above 35 years of age and below 20 years of age is much lower among the Pandits than among the Muslims, the percentage frequency of such children at Sopore is higher among the Pandits than among the Muslims. Thus the risk of genetically malformed children being produced is greater at Sopore among the Pandits than among the Muslims and at Srinagar it is greater among the Muslims than the Pandits.

Kashmiri Pandits and Muslims of Srinagar and Sopore, respectively, give the similar results when compared with respect to effect on age at marriage, duration of interval between marriage and '0' parity. Duration of married life, sex of the first two children and pre-natal and post-natal deaths respectively suffered at first and/or second conceptions, respectively, upon the fertility performances of the women.

Lastly, in an attempt to assess the trend of growth rate in terms of net increase in family size over one and a half decade of Pandit and Muslim populations of Srinagar and Sopore respectively, it is observed that Muslims have had a much greater rise in the growth rate than the Pandits of these areas.

Fertility and Body Dimensions

Study was conducted to understand the association, if any, that may exist between fertility and body dimensions of the Kashmiri Pandit women and of the Kashmiri Muslim women respectively.

Among the Kashmiri women (both Pandits and Muslims), stature seems to play an important role in determining the fertility and bears a reciprocal relationship with fertility with the shorter statured women being more fertile than the taller women. There is a tendency of negative relationship between body weight and fertility with stocky women being more fertile than the lean women. No generalized trend of relationship between fertility and chest and hip girths respectively, is discernible with respect to the chest and hip girths, the Pandit women with higher fertility show somewhat broader chest and wider hips than the Muslim women with higher fertility, who show somewhat narrower chests and hips compared to the respective women of lower fertility.

No specific relationship is discernible between fertility and calf girth. However, women with greater maximum upper arm girth were found to have a tendency of being less fertile.

No significant trend was observed in case of sub-cutaneous fat at biceps and at triceps, respectively, *vis-a-vis* fertility. Also no significant association is seen between the muscle and bone content and the fertility.

Fertility and Physique—an inter population comparison of Pandits and Muslims

Finally, an attempt has been made to make the inter-population comparison of Kashmiri Pandits and Kashmiri Muslims with

De Camargo, C. P. F., Berquo, E. S., Patarra, N. L., Levy, M. S. F., Szmroosanyi, M. I. Q. F. and Renner, C.H.O. 1970. Marriage, patterns and fertility in Sao Pauolo. *Social Biology*, 17(4), 260-268.

Desai, P. B. 1969. Size and sex composition of populations in India. Asia Publishing House, New Delhi.

Dutt, James S. 1980. Altitude and fertility: The compounding effect of childhood mortality—A Bolivian Example. *Social Biology*, 27(2), 101-113.

Eaton, J. W. and Mayor, A. J. 1953. The social biology of very high fertility among the Hutterites. *Human Biology*, 25, 206-263.

Epstein, T. S. 1975. Population Growth and its social dimensions. In the paradox of poverty—Socio-economic aspects of population growth. T. Scarlett Epstein and Darrell Jackson. The Macmillan Company of India Ltd. Delhi, 3-24.

Franklin, R. W. 1974. Perinatal mortality rates. *American Journal of Obstetrics and Gynaecology*, 119, 297-305.

Freedman, R. 1964. Population, the vital Revolution. Anchor Books edition, Doubleday and Company Inc.

Freedman, R. and Coombs, L. 1966. Childspacing and family economic position. *American Sociological Review*, 31, 631-648.

Freymann, Moyce, W. 1960. Observations in family Planning—Action Research in India's Population by S.N. Agarwala (ed.). Asia Publishing House, New Delhi, 198-208.

Frisancho, A. Roberts; Klayman, Jane E. and Matos, Jorge. 1976. Symbolic relationship of high fertility, high childhood mortality and socio-economic status in an urban Peruvian population. *Human Biology*, 48(1), 101-111.

Gandhi, L. P. 1978. Interval between age at marriage and first birth among Maheshwari community. Anthropological Survey of India, Nagpur.

George, Mollykutty. 1976. Fertility differential in a rural community. *The Journal of Family Welfare*, 22(4), 3-8.

Ghosh, B. 1975. Recent studies in social and economic determinants of fertility. *Journal of Family Welfare*. 21, 38-45.

Gini, C. 1934. Proceedings of the International Congress for studies on population, Rome, 1931. Anthropology and Geography.

Goyal, R. P. 1975. Shifts in age at marriage in India between 1961-71. *Demography in India*, 4(2), 336-344.

Grabill, W. H. and Davidson, M. 1968. Recent trends in child spacing among American women. *Demography*, 5, 212-225.

Grant, M. W. 1951. Techniques for the analysis of height and weight data in Tropical countries. Applied Nutrition Unit, Medical Research Council, London School of Hygiene and Tropical Medicine.

Greenberg, M. A., Nelson, K. E. and Carnow, B. W. 1973. A study of the relationship between sudden infant death syndrome and environmental factors. *American Journal of Edidemiology*, 95(6), 412-422.

Gupta, R. B. 1974. Variations in the age structure of Indian population during 1961-71. Demography India, 3(2), 306-314.

Gupta, R., Singh, K. L. and David, L. H. 1975. Fertility and fertility differentials in a rural area. *The Journal of Family Welfare*, 21, 3-9.

Gurumurthy, C. 1976. Fertility Differentials in Andhra. *Demography India*, 5, 153-162.

Gustafson, E. B 1969. A demographic dilemma. *Social Biology*, 16(2), 115-127.

Gustavus, S. O. and Nam, C. B. 1970. The formation and stability of ideal family size among young people. *Demography*, 7, 43-51.

Halberstein, Robert A. and Crawford, M. H. 1975. Demographic structure of transplanted Tlaxcalar Population in the valley of Mexico. *Human Biology*, 47, 201-232.

Hans Raj, 1978. Fundamentals of Demography. Surjeet Publications, Delhi.

Harter, Carl L. 1970. The fertility of sterile and sub-fecund women in New Orleans. *Social Biology*, 17(3), 195-206.

Hawley, A. H. 1959. Population composition, In the Study of population. Phillip M. Hanser and O. D. Duncan (eds.) University of Chicago Press.

Hawthern, G. 1970. The Sociology of Fertility. Collier Macmillan, London.

Heath, C. W. 1954. Physique, temperament and sex ratio. *Human Biology*, 26, 337-342.

Hernandez, D. J. 1981. A Note on measuring the independent impact of family planning programs on fertility declines. *Demography*, 18(4), 627-634.

Hillman, R. W., Slater Paul, Nelson and Marjori, J. 1970. Season of birth, parental age, menarcheal age and body form —some inter-relationship in young women. *Human Biology*, 42, 570-580.

Howells, W. 1949. Body measurements in the light of familial influences. *American Journal of Physical Anthropology*, 7, 101-108.

Howells, W. 1953. Birth Interval and Body Size. *Human Biology*, 25, 13-20.

Hsia, David Yi-Yung. 1968. Human developmental Genetics. Year Book Medical Publisher, Chicago.

Hunt Jr., Edward, E., Lessa William A. and Hicking, A. 1965. The sex ratio of live births in three Pacific Islands populations (Yap, Samoa and New Guinea). *Human Biology*, 37, 146-155.

Husain, I. Z. 1972. Educational status and differential fertility in India. In Population Analysis and Problems. Hussain (ed.) Somaiya Publishers, Bombay.

Jain, A. K. 1969. Socio-economic correlates of fecundability in a sample of Taiwanese women. *Demography*, 6, 75-90.

Jain, M. K. 1975. Growing imbalance in the sex composition of India. *Demography India*, 4(2), 305-315.

Jain, S. P. 1939. Relationship between fertility and economic and social status in the Punjab, Lahore. The Board of Economic Inquiry, Punjab Publication, 64.

James, W. H. 1975. The decline in dizygotic twinning rates and in birth rates. *Annals of Human Biology*, 2(1), 81-84.

Johnston, F E., Kensinger, K. M., Jantz, R. L. and Walker, G. F. 1969. The population structure of the Peruvian Cashinahua—demographic genetic and cultural inter-relationship. *Human Biology*, 41(1). 29-41.

Jones, D. L. 1974. Human reproduction and society. Faber and Faber, London.

Kan, Yung Sun and Cho, Wan Kyo. 1962. The Sex Ratio at birth and other attributes of the newborn from maternity hospitals in Korea. *Human Biology*, 34(1), 38-48.

Karan, P.P. and Boerner. C. 1973. Spatial patterns of Human fertility behaviour in India. *National Geography* (Allahabad) 8, 1-13.

Karim, M. S. and King, J. R. 1974. Fertility differentials by family type. *A Pakistan Demography Review* (Islamabad), 13, 129-144.

Kaul, Ikbal. 1978. Kashmiri Pandits through the ages, *Koshur Samachar*, Special Number, 53-57.

Khalifa, Atef M. 1976. The Influence of wife's education on fertility in rural Egypt. *Journal of Biosocial Science*, 8, 53-60.

Khan, M. E. 1973. Factors affecting spacing of births. *Journal of Family Welfare*, 20(2), 54-67.

King, J. R. 1974. Immigrant fertility trends and population growth in Leeds. *Env. and Plan.*, 6, 509-546.

Krishnamurthy, K. G. 1968. Research in family planning in India. Sterling Publishers, Delhi.

Kumari, J. R. and Rao, T. V. 1982. Family Planning and increased fitness of the child to survive. *Journal of Family Welfare*, 28(3), 76-81.

Lasker, G. W. and Thomas, R. 1976. Relationship between reproductive fitness and anthropometric dimensions in a Mexican population. *Human Biology*, 48(4), 775-791.

Lee, Che-Fu and Lin Kuang Hua. 1975. Conception delay, non-susceptible period and cohort fertility patterns. *Demography*, 12(1), 143-153.

Luella, Klein. 1974. Early teenage pregnancy contraception and repeat pregnancy. *American Journal of Obstetrics and Gynaecology*, 120, 249-256.

Machin, G. A. and Crolla, J. A. 1974. Chromosome constitution of Infants. *Humangenetik* (Berlin), 23(3), 183-198.

Majumdar, D. N. 1960. Social contours of an industrial city. Social survey of Kanpur, 1954-1960. Asia Publishing House, Bombay.

Memoria, C. B. 1965. Population and family planning in India. Kitabmahal, Allahabad.

Mandelbaum, D. G. 1974. Human Fertility in India. Oxford University Press, Delhi.

Martinez, M. G. 1956. Constitution humana Y determination del sexo. Editorial Litografia, Colombia.

Martorell, R., Delgado, V. V. and Klein, R. E. 1981. Maternal stature, fertility and infant mortality. *Human Biology*, 53, 303-312.

Masnick, G. S. and McFalls Jr., J. A. 1976. A new perspective on the twentieth century American fertility swing. *Journal of Fam Hist.*, 1(2), 216-243.

Matsunaga, Ei. 1969. Some reflections on the biological consequences of family planning. *Indian Journal of Medical Education*, 9, 123-126.

Matsunaga, Ei and Tonomura, A. 1972. Parental age and birth weight in translocation Down's syndrome. *Annals of Human Genetics*, 36, 209-219.

Matsunaga, Ei. 1973. Effect of changing parental age patterns in chromosomal aberrations and Mutation. *Social Biology*, 20(1), 82-88.

McAlpine, P. J. and Simpson, N. E. 1976. Fertility and other demographic aspects of the Canadian Eskimo communities of Igloolik and Hall Beach. *Human Biology*, 48(1), 113-138.

McKausick, V.A. 1972. Human Genetics. Prentice Hall of India, New Delhi.

Mitra, A. 1970. The small family norm and literacy. In Studies in demography. A. Bose, P. B. Desai and S. P. Jain (eds.). George Allen and Unwin, London.

Mitton, J. B. 1975. Fertility differentials in modern societies resulting in normalizing selection for Height. *Human Biology*, 47, 189-201.

Mo-Im, Kim, Rider, Rowland, V., Harper P. A. and Yang, Jae, Mo. 1974 Age at marriage, family planning practices and other variables as correlates of fertility in Korea. *Demography*, 11, 641-656.

Montague, F. A. 1960 An Introduction to Physical Anthropology. Charles C. Thomas Publisher, U.S.A.

Mueller, William M. 1979. Fertility and physique in a malnourished population. *Human Biology*, 51, 153-166.

Mukherjee, R. K. and Singh, E. 1961. Social profiles of a metropolis. Bombay. Asia Publishing House.

Mukherjee, S. B. 1962. Studies on fertility rates in Calcutta. Bookland, Calcutta.

Murthy. J. S and Jain. 1972. Inbreeding load in the newborn of Hyderabad, *Acta Genetic—Medica et Gamellologiae*, 21(4), 327-331.

Natarajan, D. 1972. Extracts from the All India Census Reports on Literacy, Census of India. 1971. Census Centenary Monograph No. 9, New Delhi.

National Sample Survey. 1963. Fertility and Mortality Rates in India. Report No. 76, New Delhi, Manager of Publications.

Nayar, P. K. B. 1974. The influence of education on fertility. *Journal of Family Welfare*, 20, 28-36.

Naylor, A. F. 1974. Sequential aspects of spontaneous abortions —maternal age, parity and pregnancy compensation artifact. *Social Biology*, 21(2), 195-204.

Neel, J. and Weiss, K. 1975. The Genetic structure of a tribal population—the yanomana Indians. *American Journal of Physical Anthropology*, 42(1), 25-32.

New Ombe, H. B. 1964. Screening for effects of maternal age and birth order in a register of handicapped children. *Annals of Human Genetics*, 27, 357-362.

Norland (Yan) J. A. 1975. Measuring change in sex composition. *Demography*, 12(1), 81-88.

Novitsky, E. and Kimball, A. W. 1958. Birth order, parental ages and sex of offsprings. *American Journal of Human Genetics*, 10, 268-275.

Oliveira, Adelia E. and Sakzano, F. M. 1969. Genetic implications of the Demography of Brazilian Juruna Indians. *Social Biology*, 16(2), 209-285.

Pareek, U. and Kothandapani, V. 1969. Modernization and attitude to family size and family planning. *Social Biology*, 16(1), 44-48.

Parnell, R.W. 1958. Behaviour and physique. Edward Arnold, London.

Penrose, L. S. 1964. Review of Court Brown's abnormalities of the sex chromosome complement in Mem. *Annals of Human Genetics*, 28, 199-200.

Philippe, P. 1974. Amenorrhea, intrauterine mortality and parental consanguinity in an isolated French population. *Human Biology*, 46(3), 405-424.

Poti, S. J. and Dutta, S. 1958. Pilot study on social mobility and differential fertility. Indian Statistical Institute, Calcutta.

Presser, H. B. 1971. The timing of the first birth, female roles and black fertility. *Milbank Memorial Fund Quarterly*, 49, 329-362.

Potter, R. G., Ford, K. and Moots, B. 1975. Competition between spontaneous and induced abortions. *Demography*, 12(1), 129-141.

Raina, B. L. 1969 Family size norms in population problems in India. Central Family Planning Institute.

Rakshit, S. 1962. Reproductive life of some Maharashtrian Brahmin women. *Man in India*, 42, 139-159.

Ram, E. R. and Dutta, B. 1976 Differential fertility in a rural area. *Demography India*, 5(1 & 2), 144-153.

Ray, S. C. 1957. Early history and culture of Kashmir, U. N. Dhar & Sons. Calcutta.

Resseguie, L. S. 1974. Pregnancy wastage and age of mother among the Amish. *Human Biology*, 46(4), 633-639.

Ritchey, P. N. 1973. Effects of marital status on the fertility of rural urban and urban-rural migrants. *Rural Sociology*, 38(1), 26-35.

Roberts, C. J. and Lowo, C. R. 1975. "Where have all the conceptions gone ?" *Larcet No. 7905*, 498-499.

Roy, S. and Ghosh, A. K. 1972. Family welfare planning : Its genetic considerations. International Conference of Family Planning, New Delhi.

Selvin, Steve and Garfinkel, Joseph. 1972. The relationship between parental age and birth order with the percentage of low birth weight infants. *Human Biology*, 44(3), 501-510.

Selvin, S. and Garfinkel, J. 1976. Paternal age, maternal age and birth order and the risk of a foetal loss. *Human Biology*, 48(1), 223-230.

Scott-Emuakpor, Ajovi B. 1974. The mutation load in an African population an analysis of consanguineous marriage in Nigeria. *American Journal of Human Genetics*, 26(6), 674-682.

Shryock, H. S. and Siegel J. S. 1971. The methods and materials of Demography. Academic Press, New York.

Singh, I. P. and Bhasin, M. K. 1968. Anthropometry. Bharti Bhawan, Delhi.

Singh, K. P. 1974. Child mortality, social status and fertility in India. *Social Biology*, 21(4), 385-388.

Sinha, J. N. 1957. Differential fertility and family limitation in an urban community of U. P. *Population Studies*, 11(2), 157-169.

Sovani, N. V. 1948. The social survey of Kolhapur city, Part I population and fertility. Gokhale Institute of Politics and Economics, Publication No. 18, Poona.

Sovani, N. V. and Dandekar, K. 1955. Fertility survey of Nasik, Kolaba and Satara Districts. Gokhale Institute of Politics and Economics. Pub. No. 31, Poona.

Spiers, P. S. 1974. Estimated rates of concordancy for the sudden infant death syndrome in twins. *American Journal of Epidemiology*, 100(1), 1-7.

Srikantan, K. S. and Saxena, S. 1981. Population census results in perspective. *Journal of Family Welfare*, 28(2), 5-16.

Stein, Z. and Sussex, M. 1975. Fertility, Fecundity : Famine. *Human Biology*, 47, 131-154.

Stern, C. 1968. Principles of human genetics. Eurasia Publishing House, New Delhi.

Stinner W. F. and Mader, P. D. 1975. An analysis of family sex composition preferences in the Phillipines. *Demography* 12(1), 67-69.

Stoeckel, J. and Choudhury, M. A. 1969. Knowledge and Practice of family planning in E. P. villages, *Social Biology*, 16(1), 29-38.

Stolnitz, G. J. 1964. The Demographic transition : from high to low birth rates and death rates. In Population : the vital revolution. Ronald Freeman (ed.) Anchor Books Doubleday & Co. Inc., New York, 30-46.

Strandskov, H. H. 1942. Variance of human live birth sex-ratio. *Human Biology*, 14(1), 85-94.

Stukovsky, R. 1967. Family size and menarchael age in Constanza, Romania. *Human Biology*, 39(3), 277-283.

Stycos, M. J. 1970. Education and fertility in Puerto Rico. In Social Demography. Thomas R. Ford and Gordon F. De Jong (eds).

Talwar, P. P. 1965. Adolescent sterility in an Indian population. *Human Biology*, 37, 256-261.

——. 1975. Effect of desired sex-composition in families on the birth rates. *Journal of Biosocial Science*, 7(2), 133-139.

Tanner, J.M. 1960. Genetics of human growth. Pergamon Press.

Tikkoo, P. N. 1979. Story of Kashmir. Light and Life Publishers, New Delhi.

Tiwari, K. 1974. Fertility and physique of muslim women of East Nimar. unpublished Ph. D. thesis.

Thompson, W. S. 1953. Population problems. McGraw Hill Book Company. Inc., New York.

—— and Lewis, D. T. 1965. Population problems. McGraw Hill Book Company, New York.

Treloar, A. E. 1974. Menarche, menopause and intervening fecundability. *Human Biology*, 46(1), 89-107.

Trussel, J. and Brown, E. 1979. Demography of Afghanistan. *Demography*, 16(1), 137-156.

United Nations. 1961. Mysore population study. Department of Economics and Social Welfare, New York.

——. 1966. The Mysore population study (1952), cited from Agarwala, S. N. Some Problems of India's Population, Vohra and Co. Publishers Pvt. Ltd., Bombay.

Vaidyanathan, K. E. 1967. Population redistribution and economic changes in India, 1951-61. University of Pennsylvania.

Vatwani, V. 1973. A survey of perinatal mortality in a military hospital. *AFM Journal*, 29(1), 38-49.

Veevers, J. E. 1973. Rural-urban differences in the distribution of birth orders. *Rural Sociology*, 38(2), 219-227.

Verbrugge, L. M. 1976. Sex differentials in the morbidity and mortality in the USA. *Social Biology*, 23(4), 275-296.

Vetta, A. 1975. Fertility, physique and intensity of selection. *Human Biology*, 47, 283-293.

Vogel, H. P. and Knox, F. G. 1975. Reproductive patterns after still birth and early infant death. *Journal of Biosocial Science*, 7(2), 103-111.

Vig. C. P 1976. India's population—A study through extension of stable population technique. Sterling Publishers Pvt. Ltd., New Delhi.

Vital Statistics of India. 1972. Office of the Registrar General, India, Ministry of Home Affairs, New Delhi.

Wattal, P. K. 1958. Population Problem in India : A census stuy. Minerva Book Shop, Simla.

Williamson, N. E. 1980. Utilizing research to manage a family planning project. *Studies in Family Planning* 11 (9 & 10).

Working Group on Population Policy, Interim Report, 1979. Planning Commission, Government of India.

World Health Organization, 1974. Annual global data on mortality, 1970-72. *World Health Statistical Report*, 27(5). 196-199.

Wright, N. H. 1975. Family planning and infant mortality rate decline in the U.S.A. *American Journal of Epidemiology*, 101(3), 182-187.

Yasuda, N. 1975. The distribution of distance between birth places of mates. *Human Biology*, 47(1), 81-100.

Yerushalmy, J. 1945. On the interval between successive birth and its effect on survival of infant. *Human Biology*, 17(2), 65-106.

Index